A DOG'S LIFE IN THE DALES

KATY CROPPER

A Dog's Life in The Dales

WITH BARBARA COLLINS

BANTAM BOOKS
TORONTO · NEW YORK · LONDON · SYDNEY · AUCKLAND

A DOG'S LIFE IN THE DALES
A BANTAM BOOK 0 553 40638 8

Originally published in Great Britain by Smith Gryphon Ltd

PRINTING HISTORY
Smith Gryphon edition published 1992
Bantam edition published 1993

Bantam Books are published by Transworld Publishers Ltd,
61–63 Uxbridge Road, Ealing, London W5 5SA,
in Australia by Transworld Publishers (Australia) Pty Ltd,
15–25 Helles Avenue, Moorebank, NSW 2170,
and in New Zealand by Transworld Publishers (NZ) Ltd,
3 William Pickering Drive, Albany, Auckland.

Printed and bound in Great Britain by
Cox & Wyman Ltd, Reading, Berks.

CONTENTS

To the memory of Susie

ACKNOWLEDGEMENTS

The help extended to me by the people who appear in this book has been tremendous; others from the sheepdog and farming world have also been unstinting in their encouragement and comment — my thanks to them all.

In particular, I would like to thank Kath Cooper for reading the first draft of the book and making appropriate comments; veterinary surgeons Adam Hurn, David Metcalfe and Gerry Hayhurst for the supply of veterinary information; Roger Scruton and Richard Fawcett for their photography, and other photographers, some of them anonymous, who have made a contribution; *Working Sheepdog News* for kindly giving me permission to use some of my early cartoons which were previously published in the magazine.

Above all, I would like to thank Barbara Collins without whose help this book might never have been written.

A flock of sheep that leisurely pass by,
One after one; the sound of rain, and bees
Murmuring; the fall of rivers, winds and seas,
Smooth fields, white sheets of water, and pure sky.

WILLIAM WORDSWORTH

INTRODUCTION

Animals have always played a major part in my life. My childhood was filled with a motley collection of living creatures which I tended and cherished with loving attention — I kept them clean and sweet-smelling, fed them with care, groomed their coats, read every book I could find on the specific breeds, loved them fiercely and enjoyed the reward of their company and affection. My ponies and I had years of fun together when hacking in the local countryside or competing at gymkhanas, and at one time I even had an imaginary zoo in the back garden, filled with various exotic animals which would have been impractical to keep in any other way. I am not from an agricultural background, so my contact with farm animals began on family holidays spent on farms. Later, local farmers welcomed me on to their land to help with tending their stock, and this eventually led, in adult life, to my work as a shepherdess and the training and handling of working Border Collies.

To say that I am besotted with sheep and sheepdogs would be an understatement. My Border Collies are all from working stock and are registered in the Stud Book of the International Sheepdog Society; they are my workmates and constant companions, and it is now impossible to imagine life without them. Learning to train and handle these intelligent, brave dogs has given me hours of pleasure, some pain and not a little terror when I began to compete at sheepdog trials — a mere unknown and a woman at that! But I will be eternally grateful to all those sheepdog people who have given me their friendship, tuition and advice — without them, I would never have been able to reach the standard of handling which enabled me to become the first woman to win the *One Man and His Dog* championship in 1990, an achievement of which I will always be proud.

Over the years I have grown to love sheep, and, having experimented with different breeds, I am now the proud owner of some registered Swaledales. With their long, wavy fleeces, curved horns and bonny faces, these sheep have become my favourites. I have joined the Swaledale Breeders' Association in the hope that one day my small flock will produce a tup — a ram (the glossary on p. 199 explains a lot of sheep and sheepdog terms) — or ewe good enough to show at Tan Hill, which is one of the most prestigious Swaledale sheep shows in England.

Wensleydale, in North Yorkshire, has been my home since the late 1980s. To me it is a magical place which never fails to keep me spellbound, whatever the season or weather, drawing me back time and again to its high fells and lonely places. Now, looking back over my thirty-one years, I know that this time spent in the fastness of the Yorkshire Dales has been the happiest of my life, for I was a wild child and young adult who seemed unable to settle anywhere before living and working in this wild and beautiful place.

My introduction to the area came when I went to work for Richard and Anne Fawcett as lambing assistant on their farm at Hardraw, and as part-time nanny to their four children, Hannah, Ruth, Jane and Joshua. I still work there, with the highlight of the year being the seven weeks of lambing time, which I love. In addition I now help both Richard and his cousin John (whose farm lies a mile down the road from Richard's) with shepherding work throughout the year. As a result, my knowledge of sheep and the shepherd's task has grown apace.

Richard has been a hard but fair task-master, from the time when he bluntly announced that until I could get inside a sheep's head I would never be able to anticipate its movements, up to the present time when any mistakes I make during my work are carefully analysed and alternatives offered. All this has increased my confidence when working with the sheep and my dogs, and has certainly contributed to my growing success when competing in sheepdog trials, where sheep lore is as important as the ability to handle a dog.

As my friendship with Richard and Anne has grown, they have encouraged me not only to continue to develop my commitment to shepherding, but also to have the confidence to branch out and use my skills in other ways. So now, in addition to training and handling my own sheepdogs, I am helping others to improve their handling skills by running local sheepdog training classes for the Agricultural Training Board; I train dogs for other people; I continue to compete in sheepdog trials; and I demonstrate with my dogs, sheep and ducks all over the British Isles at agricultural and other shows. Latterly I have, to my surprise, taken up after-dinner speaking.

Although I have a solitary side to my personality which enables me to enjoy the life of a shepherdess, I have always been a bit of a show-off when in company, and the aspects of my work which take me to far-flung places fulfil my sporadic need for an audience. I love the countryside and the animals, but I need a regular input of bright lights and different people around me, so I consider myself lucky because I seem to be getting the best of both worlds. However, the gregarious life soon begins to pall, and then I head back for the peace and beauty of the place that is now my home.

KATY CROPPER
SEDBUSK
1992

1

A BORN MAVERICK

One of the best times in the Dales begins for me in the autumn, when the holidaymakers and walkers have gone home and the whole place belongs once more to the locals, their animals, the wildlife and the weather. That is when I can take some time off work and, with my sheepdogs at my side, set off to explore the silence and wildness of the countryside, looking, learning, storing up my growing knowledge of the area and adding to my memories.

The dogs and I love to walk over the tops from Hardraw to Thwaite at the top of Swaledale. The distance is about six miles, going up the Pennine Way over the huge landmarks of Blea Pot and Great Shunner Fell, with superb views which will stay in my mind forever, no matter how far from the Dales I might travel in the future. A paradise in the summer months with sweet smells, curlews crying, deep gills full of sparkling water, springy grass and wilderness, it is nothing short of heaven on a crisp, bright winter's day. Reaching the top of Great Shunner Fell at 2349 feet I can look back to the view which stretches to the east down the length of Wensleydale. Southwards lies Widdale, between the tops of Widdale Fell and Snaizeholme Fell; and, due south, I can see the beloved Dodd Fell on which I spend so much of my working time. This fell surrounds the valley of Sleddale and ends in the southern peak (known locally as the Crown) of Dodd Fell Hill, which at 2204 feet is only slightly lower than the point on which I am standing. In the near distance to the south, the land drops down into the narrow valley of Cotterdale, with Abbotside Common and Lund's Fell towering behind it. Cotterdale is my idea of the perfect dale. Tucked snugly between the fells, and utterly quiet and peaceful with a beck running down to the waterfall known as Cotter Force, it is a place where you might be lucky enough to see the occasional roe deer, kestrel, sparrowhawk or heavy barn owl. The central, lower part of Cotterdale is surrounded by belts of conifers which provide a visual contrast to the starkness of the surrounding hills, offering dark shelter to wildlife.

Continuing up and over the top, the sights are equally spectacular on the other side. After leaving Thwaite behind me, I drop further down into Swaledale. Looking back to Black Hill and Black Bank on Thwaite Common, just below Great Shunner Fell, I know that, in this high country, I can be completely at peace, with no sound but the dogs' paws and my boots crunching on the snowy ground. These are the times when I do a lot of my thinking — not only about the present, but also about my childhood, adolescence and early twenties when life often seemed confusing, tumultuous and unhappy, even though it was peppered with good times. I have always needed wide, open spaces and the silence which surrounds them, and I increasingly use these solitary times to tease out problems, weigh up situations and make decisions. Whenever I have been away from home, the first thing I do is put on my boots and go out on to the fells with the dogs. Only then can I feel myself relax as I adjust back to the reality, the hardship, the down-to-earth people and the pleasures of country living.

I now live in Lilac Cottage in the village of Sedbusk, which is about two miles from the Green Dragon public house at Hardraw. Behind the pub is the path which leads to Hardraw Force; after heavy autumn rain I and my dogs wander up it and through an eerie ravine to see the great waterfall which tumbles over Hardraw Scar with terrifying power. I stand behind the falls, mesmerized by the torrents of water thundering above me; the sound is incredible. It is times like these which fill me with pure joy and I feel immensely close to God. As a child, I was somewhat over-fed with Christianity by well-meaning family and friends, almost putting me off the poor chap for good; but now I know, as I enjoy the beauty of the Dales, that they could only have been created by a divine hand.

Swaledale ewe and Lamb

After the relative tranquillity of winter, it is hard work again in the spring for the sheep farmers of the Dales. At The Croft, Richard Fawcett's farm, I assist with the lambing of six hundred Swaledale ewes. There is no doubt that this is the favourite of all my shepherding tasks — it is also the busiest time, when I get short on sleep and long on walking. By the third week in March, all the ewes have been gathered and brought down from the heights of Dodd Fell to the home fields, which are enclosed by well-kept dry-stone walls to keep the flocks in and give the sheep and lambs shelter from the weather. Some of these fields also contain old stone barns which can be put to use as additional shelter when the weather turns really bad; and, for sick sheep, there are always the straw-lined pens we put up in the silage barn, which is almost empty by this time of the year.

When the lambs begin to arrive, the ewes with a single lamb are left in the fields but those with twins are brought under cover for twelve to twenty-four hours to ensure that mothering-up takes place, that there is plenty of milk in the ewe's udder, and that the lambs get a good start. We also have fostering pens which are used to foster an orphan lamb on to a ewe who has lost her own offspring. So the silage barn becomes a hive of activity and hard work, with one shepherd always on duty in there day and night to ensure that nothing goes wrong.

At lambing time I get up at dawn, take a couple of my dogs and walk round the fields until darkness falls again, to check the flocks and watch for ewes which might be in need of help when giving birth. Whenever there is a lull in this work, there are all the other tasks to be seen to: marking, castrating, feeding sickly lambs, taking ewes with twins to the silage barn, fostering orphans on to new mums, injecting ewes for calcium shortage, moving ewes who have already given birth out of the lambing fields to other pastures, and watching for mis-mothering – the stealing of lambs by pregnant ewes. In addition, we constantly refill the hayracks and feed the flock with ewe and lamb nuts throughout the lambing weeks – this continues for two to three weeks afterwards and helps to keep the sheep in good condition.

Although we are usually able to help a ewe to lamb successfully when things are going wrong, some lambs are stillborn. Then there is occasionally what we call a 'water-bellied' lamb (the lamb is full of fluid, making it too large to get through the birth canal). This means it has to be killed to drain the fluid before we can get the pathetic little body out and save the life of the mother. Sometimes one or both of a lamb's legs, instead of coming out of the uterus first, are lying back inside the womb. This causes swelling of the lamb's head, but fortunately these cases can usually be saved if we reach them in time, and the swelling soon goes down after the lambs are born. If a lamb is lost there is always a feeling of sadness at a small life wasted, but this gradually disappears as the busy routine continues and the count of healthy, live births increases.

It was during my first lambing at Hardraw that I thought a lamb had returned miraculously to life. Richard had left a note asking me to bring in a ewe and put her in the fostering pens to have another lamb fostered on to her because her own offspring was dead. He wrote that he had tied some string on her horns to identify the ewe and that she was 'in the lambing field'. As is customary in most farming communities, every field has a name to differentiate it from the others. On this occasion, I automatically went to the field where we were lambing the ewes — the lambing field — despite the fact that the proper name for that field is the Golf Links. And, sure enough, there was the ewe with string on her horns — with a live lamb at foot! I rushed to find Richard to tell him the wonderful news, only to find that I had gone to the wrong field and found a ewe which had been marked for a different reason. Richard had meant 'Lambing Field', which is the proper name for one of the fields away from the lambing area. It gets very complicated at times.

One of the saddest and most unpleasant tasks for any shepherd during these busy weeks is having to bury the small carcasses of dead lambs. They look so sad and defenceless that no shepherd can remain unmoved when he does this job. But fortunately deaths are few and far between in Richard's flock, because he demands a very high standard of care and stockmanship throughout the year. It pays off at lambing time.

When I cross the paddock near the house, after doing my rounds and before breakfast, I can hear the familiar sound of machinery starting up. So I poke my head round the sliding door of the milking parlour to say good morning to Jack — a great character and a true Dalesman who has worked for Richard and his father, Dick, for forty-two years with hardly a day's work lost in all that time.

'Art ee all reet, Kate?' he shouts from behind a cow's udder. Four years after arriving here I have just about got the gist of what he is saying. Jack and I are the best of friends most of the time, but I am not always popular with him — and for good reason. There was the occasion when I drove the Land Rover over his old farm bike; he had to walk everywhere after that and told me he was really 'twined' with me. The worst times are when I have done something which makes him chunter under his breath or shout, as happens when he suddenly comes across the female lambs called hoggs, which I use for training the young dogs,

milking time

grazing in fields where the grass is being saved for his precious cows.

'Git them yowes out of yon fog, yer nowt but a blasted nuisance, you sheepdog folk!' yells Jack, and I feel I could curl up and die. He is in a bit of a mood with me at the moment because I borrowed his favourite hand-shears and have forgotten where I left them. They are lovely little clippers which he uses to trim the cows' tails, and I have found them ideal for hand-shearing my own sheep and for dagging the flock – cutting the wool round the rump. I will have to do my best to find them. I give Jack my most brilliant smile and hope that he will forgive me, guessing that, when lambing time is over, we two country people will have a pint together at the Green Dragon and laugh about it all.

My love of the countryside dates back to the time when my parents went to live in North Wales. I was four years old when Dad founded St David's College at Gloddaeth Hall near Llandudno, only a few miles away from the mountains of Snowdonia. The college buildings stand on high ground at the back of the town, giving views of the mountains which could be seen from our sitting room. As I grew older, Dad would take me for long walks up there — Moel Siabod, to the south of the village of Capel Curig, was our favourite mountain. When we reached the top at 2861 feet we had the most amazing views of the Snowdon massif, the rivers, peaks, mountain passes and lakes which abound there, and, of course, the sea to the north, west and south of us. Due west, we could see the island of Anglesey lying just beyond the narrow Menai Strait which separates it from the mainland, and beyond that, on a clear day, the coastline of Ireland. To the south was Cardigan Bay, bounded on its north-west side by the arm of the Lleyn peninsula and to the east by the coastline of mid-Wales — another wild, mountainous region which I love.

Now, whenever I drive into North Wales, my affection for the place comes rushing back and, with it, a hotchpotch of memories from childhood and early adult life. I can vividly remember those who peopled my existence at that time, who have had a lasting influence — for better or for worse — and who had to cope with a fiery, naughty, disruptive little termagant in their midst. Always a tomboy, I was the despair of my parents and the only one of their five children who consistently refused to conform to middle-class *mores*. My end-of-term school reports were always revealing and consisted almost exclusively of comments such as 'Lacks concentration'; 'Untidy — a disgrace to herself and the school'; 'Makes no effort in work she does not enjoy'; 'Erratic'; 'Disruptive'; 'Talkative'; 'Cheerful, extrovert and lively' (I liked this one); 'Distracting antics in class'. Other remarks reflected my passionate interest in and love of animals: 'Keeps writing about horses'; 'Learns well when animals are the subject but finds plant biology of little interest'.

I was a disaster in the domestic science class — the height of my achievement being when I made Scotch eggs and failed to shell the hard-boiled eggs before wrapping them in sausage meat — but I did quite well in art, for which I had a natural flair. The only eulogies I received during my time at Penrhos College for Girls were from the sports department. I enjoyed all sports and athletics, worked very hard to become proficient, and won awards from the school, the Amateur

Athletic Association, the British Amateur Gymnastics Association, various running clubs and cross-country riding clubs. I broke a few running records — one being the Penrhos College 1500 metres, which was beaten only recently — and I ran for Clwyd County. I also represented my school in the Junior Judo Championships at home and abroad. So, although my academic achievements were low, I became a star pupil in sport — which seemed far more important to me.

I am not so proud of my behaviour when, in my teens, I went to France to compete in the judo championships. I hated learning French, and the fact that I was staying with a French family did little to improve my knowledge of the language (one of the reasons for going there) because I consistently refused to speak anything but English. Before I went to France I had discovered that they ate horsemeat, a habit which seemed preposterous to me because horses were my friends. I therefore always viewed French food with suspicion — a feeling fostered by the occasion when, their dog having chased and killed the neighbour's pet rabbit, my hosts served up the poor creature for dinner. I do remember one moment of triumph when I was competing against a French girl who was several grades higher in the sport than me — I won the bout by throwing her right out of the ring in a very unsporting manner, and I can recall the feeling of satisfaction I experienced when she crashed against the table on which the trophies were standing, knocking them all flying. But I returned from my sorties to France without adding to my French vocabulary in the slightest. Now I wish that I had not behaved like a spoilt little brat there, because I think a second language is a useful asset in this cosmopolitan age and I missed my chance.

Dad has always been interested in sport, and to this day still exhausts himself when watching a game of rugby on television — he shouts and roars with the best of them. His enthusiasm is infectious, and when I am in the house with him we have yelled ourselves hoarse by the end of the match. Dad always gave me coaching and encouragement in all my athletic activities, shouting from the sidelines when I was competing. I think I gave him some satisfaction from these achievements, even though I have always felt I let my parents down badly by not being more of an academic. Having inherited a passion for rugby (one of my sports teachers once made the comment: 'She plays netball as though it was a game of rugby') I decided, at the age of fourteen, that I wanted to go to Cardiff Arms Park to watch the match between England and Wales. Dad forbade me to go because he was worried in case I was unable to get into the ground; but, true to form, his refusal made little impression on my wayward mind. I hopped on the train, carrying a giant leek emblem which I had made the night before, and managed to buy a ticket for the match from one of the touts. The first thing Dad knew about it all was when he was watching the match on television; the camera zoomed in on part of the crowd, and there was I, leaping about with excitement and brandishing my leek! We can laugh together about it now, but he was less than pleased with me at the time.

The other major interest in my life at this time was animals. Although our back garden contained a collection of different-sized hutches housing various rabbits and guinea pigs which multiplied with surprising frequency, there could never be enough of them to satisfy my insatiable need for livestock. So I built up an imaginary zoo, using a disused greenhouse and a shed to provide shelter for my illusory animals. Looking back, I remember there were no lions or tigers but I did have a kangaroo, an owl, a polar bear, a hippopotamus and a duck-billed platypus. But it was the hyena which gave me the most pleasure, and I would join in its imagined laughter, driving my mother up the wall with irritation and probably more than a little worry each time she found her daughter laughing hysterically with no apparent cause.

I once had an open day at this zoo, charging an entrance fee to all the neighbourhood children who came to see it. I placed my younger sister, Ali, at the gate with her plastic toy till and left her in charge of the money. Everybody was cross with me when they were unable to find the animals I had been telling them about. The first thing Mum and Dad knew about it all was when the children's parents came round to the house to complain and to demand the money back. Not surprisingly, my parents were furious about the whole episode and I was in disgrace for a while. But this did nothing to quash my imagination — I just kept quiet about the zoo after that, and stopped inviting people to admire my latest (imaginary) acquisitions.

It was shortly after this episode that my mother and I were walking to Penrhos Junior School one day and saw, with some surprise, a real, live alligator walking across the road. Mum phoned the police to tell them, but by that time everybody had heard about the escapade with my imaginary zoo. The policeman on the other end of the line took some persuading that Mum was serious, and it was only when Colwyn Bay Zoo reported that one of their alligators had escaped that the police were prepared to take any action. My schoolfriends never did believe my story, but perhaps that was hardly surprising in the circumstances.

In my real world I spent time learning how to handle and look after animals, and Mum always encouraged us children with our pets. I think she rather enjoyed them herself — with the exception of my ponies — and after we all left home she kept the small animals going for a long time. I can remember my birthdays and Christmases, too, when there were always greetings cards to me from my animals — written with loving care by my mother, although it was some time before I cottoned on. Even then, the tradition continued.

My parents always had a dog around the place, usually a Labrador, although they now have an Irish Setter which, as with all the dogs they have ever owned, completely rules the roost. For some reason my mother has never liked cats, and I appear to have inherited her attitude to them — although they look furry and cuddly, they always seem to dig their claws into the tenderest parts of my anatomy when they jump on to my knee and start to purr. But having said that, I must admit to a sneaking liking for Hardy, my present next-door neighbour's cat. He is big, black, talks all the time and is famous for following his mistress, Maureen, everywhere. One dark night I was driving down to the local market town of Hawes when I heard a loud miaow from behind my seat, where Hardy had been taking a crafty snooze. He gave me such a fright that I drove straight into a wall. Hardy, quite unconcerned, climbed on to my lap, purring, so I just sat there in my dented car, quietly stroking the cat until I had calmed down again. I admire the beauty of cats from afar, but have no desire to own one — perhaps that explains why I had no big cats in my zoo. Dogs, however, are a different thing altogether and I will come back to them later.

When I was four I was taught to ride at a local riding school in Wales, and so began a love affair with ponies and horses which only abated in my early twenties when I started to train sheepdogs. My riding teacher was called Bessie Roberts, and the pony on which I learned to ride was named Bingo. He was over thirty years old when he died in 1991, only two weeks after Bessie herself was buried — a strange coincidence.

While a new home was being built for my parents in the grounds of the school, we stayed in a house in the town of Llandudno. It was while we were there that I managed to get some useful but illicit riding experience. At the end of the road was a field containing a mule and some ponies, and I would get up in the middle of the night to ride round the field. I simply threw a rope around the neck of one of them and galloped bareback over the field as fast as it would go — one of the most exhilarating experiences I can remember. One night I persuaded Ali to go with me and, for some unexplained reason, the mule walked over to her and sank his teeth into her chest. Of course, Mum eventually saw the bite and wondered where it had come from; but I denied any knowledge of it and, being a born bossy-boots, frightened Ali into keeping her mouth shut. Eventually, Mum caught me sneaking out in my pyjamas — that put a sudden end to my nocturnal trips.

At this time, when I had little contact with horses, I remedied the situation by having two fictitious horses in my zoo. One was a lightweight cob on which I went hunting, and the other a heavy farm horse — a Suffolk Punch with a handsome head and broad chest. I used to take this imaginary beast out to the fields where I spent many happy hours ploughing imaginary straight furrows, winning imaginary ploughing contests (I still have the trophies!) and leading him back home to his imaginary, spotlessly clean shed. Looking back, it is hardly surprising that I was considered rather odd by adults who were concerned for my welfare. But at the time I was unaware of this, being fully occupied with my various pursuits, both real and in the mind.

When we eventually moved into the new house my parents bought me a pony of my own. He was a little bay called Peter Pan and he looked beautiful, but his appearance belied his temperament and he would take off down the road at full gallop, frightening me to death and causing me to lose my nerve for a time. I eventually gave up riding him, so he was sold and replaced by a Shetland pony called Happy who lived up to his name. Then, with my nerve completely restored, I acquired a pony called Silver, followed in turn by Starlight, Shane and Hannibal Hayes. I never managed to shine at showjumping, although I had set my sights on it, but I loved gymkhana events and did well at racing, galloping full pelt from start to finish.

We all go through strange phases while we are growing up. It was

Starlight

around this time that I decided I was suffering from appendicitis, not because I had a pain but because I thought that the human appendix, if left to fester, could explode, causing terrible agony and death. I continually complained of stomach pains and must have been convincing because Mum went back and forth to the doctor with me, listing my complaints, my lack of appetite, the fact that I never seemed really well. I was already refusing to eat pheasant, rabbit and anything I thought might be horsemeat, and now I stopped eating all fruit which contained pips in case they became stuck in my appendix and made the inflammation worse. In the end, the doctor suggested I should go into hospital for 'tests and observation'. This terrifying event cured me of appendicitis forever, as I am sure our astute doctor had guessed it would. By the time I had had various tubes pushed into most of my orifices I was only too glad to return home and forget all about the condition of my appendix.

As I grew older and began to get interested in boys, I would tell my parents I was going out for a ride, but take my pony into the woods to meet the latest boyfriend. Then I would ride back home, trying to look innocent of all deceit. I discovered years later that my parents had guessed what I was up to all the time — hence their attempts to introduce me to 'nice' boys at Bible-reading classes. I found most of these boys dull and uninteresting, so I would soon revert to selecting my own male friends, however unsuitable they might seem to the adults in my life. I can hear Dad saying to me, 'Why do you only attract the naughty boys?' This was a question which I was never able to answer.

My passion for riding was not restricted just to horses. Donkeys have always been special to me — they seem to have great wisdom and thoughtfulness, and the fact that Christ used to ride on a donkey always impressed me when I was a child, so that probably has something to do with it too. In the school holidays I would go down to Llandudno beach to help Mr Hughes, the donkey man, give rides to children. Years later, when I was living on Anglesey, he gave me two retired donkeys to look after. They are still there to this day, living out a comfortable, well-fed old age. Another donkey, whom I had acquired in earlier days, was called Eeyore. At that time I used to go over to help on a farm belonging to a Mr Davies, and one day, as I was bringing in the cows for milking, I spotted an old, grey donkey caught up in some barbed wire. As with any animal I came across in those days, I wanted to take it home with me to be cosseted and cared for. I asked his owner if he was prepared to sell me the donkey. He said the price was £10 — a small fortune to a ten-year-old. I rushed home and asked Mum if she would lend me the money, promising faithfully to repay her as soon as I could.

I came home with Eeyore, but as far as I can remember I never paid my mother back. More importantly, perhaps, I never gave her credit for her extreme generosity of spirit, because she was always prepared to tolerate my love of anything horsey, even though she herself was quietly terrified of the animals. She even went down into Llandudno to collect Eeyore one day when I was at school; he had escaped from his paddock and a lady telephoned to say he was in her garden eating the roses, so Mum bravely took herself off to lead him all the way back home. I never realized at the time what courage this must have taken, because a fear of horses and their ilk was beyond my comprehension in those days.

As a child I spent much of my spare time on Mr Davies's farm. My favourite task there was to clean out the housing used for his animals, getting it all sweet and fresh-smelling, with a heap of clean bedding and feed to finish it all off. To this day I still find this a most rewarding task with my own animals and never begrudge the time it all takes; I love to see the pleasure they get from good food and a fresh bed — after all, human beings appreciate these comforts, so why not animals?

Although I neglected my academic studies throughout my childhood, refusing to accept the daily grind, boredom and discipline involved, nothing could deter me from the hard work and commitment required when caring for animals — my own and other people's. The fact that this was recognized and encouraged by my parents and local farmers enabled me to begin the development of an understanding of farming, animals, the countryside and its people which eventually led me to the satisfying work in which I am now involved.

During the past few years, I have been able to get closer to my parents than I ever felt able to do as a child and, now that I can look back more objectively, I realize the enormity of the task they took on when in 1964 they first went to Gloddaeth Hall to found St David's. It was at a time when many such establishments were having a struggle to survive, and I have enormous respect for their achievement in eventually making it into one of the best boys' schools in the country. Inevitably, their complete absorption in the work they were doing meant that they had less time to spend with their own children. This is probably why I became so attached to the woman who was to become my anchor in life until her untimely death in 1979.

Patricia Wright (always Trish to me and the family) was a Norland-trained nanny who had previously cared for the children of Peter Ustinov. She entered my world when I was a baby, also taking Alison under her wing when she arrived a year later, and moving to Llandudno with us three years after that. By this time my older brother, Roger, and older sisters, Rosemary (Mo) and Susan, were at boarding school: they seemed distant and very grown-up to me. Roger was the quiet, studious member of the family — a brilliant piano player who was obsessed with cars and had no time for younger sisters. Mo and Sue were above playing with a sibling so much younger than they were; to my disgust, they tended either to boss me about or to ignore me altogether when they impinged on my life in the school holidays.

Everything about Trish was larger than life. She was a very big lady with a large bosom, a heart to match, a loud, sonorous voice, a sincere and unshakeable belief in God, and a pronounced wheeze — she suffered from asthma and always carried one of those little inhalers around with her. She had great enthusiasms for people, had definite (and not always complimentary) ideas about politicians, was a great fan of Spike Milligan and indulged a lifelong passion for liquorice. To my delight, Trish adored me from the moment she first saw me and I was always her favourite — a fact which I mercilessly used to my advantage at every opportunity throughout the years.

In addition to having responsibility for my younger sister and me, Trish also took on the job of school matron, always supporting my parents in their work and wielding quite an influence amongst boys and staff alike. One of her failings was her propensity to have favourites — if you were in with Trish, she could never do enough for you; but if she disliked you she could make life unbearable, as some of the boys (and their teachers) discovered to their cost. The strange thing was that, despite her idiosyncrasies, everybody loved Trish because she was a good sport and could always take a joke against herself. When I started at day school she would come to collect me on her old motor scooter; often, the boys would put a cardboard sign on the back of her vehicle saying 'Wide load' or 'The Tank', which was her nickname at the school. I think she secretly enjoyed the notoriety these labels gave her, because they were sometimes left on the scooter for quite a long time and she never bore malice against the perpetrators.

In the annual St David's school photographs during Trish's time she can always be seen in the front row, flanked by boys and staff, looking like the archetypal school matron and, in black and white, far more severe than the person I knew. Moving along the line of photographs through the years, there eventually appears the image of her beloved pet bulldog, Sykes, lying at the front of the line-up and daring the photographer to make one false move: Trish always told me that, when Sykes died, she intended to have him stuffed and mounted on a set of wheels so that she could still take him about with her; for a long time I believed her. Years later, when I acquired my first sheepdog, I named him Sykes in memory of Trish's dog, although nobody in the sheepdog world at that time could understand why I had given a working dog such an outlandish name.

At one time Trish's favourite teacher was Bob Shepton, the school chaplain, who was also in charge of outdoor pursuits at St David's and was a keen and experienced mountaineer. But Bob fell out of favour when Peter Thomas, a handsome new member of staff, arrived at the school, after which the mountaineer was largely ignored. One day Trish (who always pampered her pets) ran a hot bath for the new teacher, and, when it was ready, locked the bathroom door to prevent anybody else from grabbing the opportunity to have a long soak. Bob, finding he was unable to get into the bathroom, went upstairs, donned his mountaineering clothes and boots, and climbed down to the bathroom window from the window above. When Trish eventually unlocked the door she discovered him with his arms crossed and lying full length in the bath — still in all his climbing gear! I doubt if she ever forgave him, but I'm sure the event must have given the chaplain enormous satisfaction.

Trish was always a very honest and straightforward person, with an ability to swear profusely on occasion; she would use a random selection of barrack-room words which I found most engaging, so I stored them up for future reference. I am sure that my parents, particularly my mother, disliked this side of Trish's personality, but she seemed impervious to implied or direct criticism and continued to go her own sweet way. In any case she had become indispensable to the family and the school, and as a result managed to get away with her language lapses.

The windows of Trish's upstairs sitting room overlooked the front of the main entrance, and if I look up at them now I can still see her in my mind's eye, leaning out of the window and bellowing at some poor schoolboy (a current non-favourite) to tuck his shirt into his trousers, or to stop slouching. Her voice would boom around the playing fields, seeping into every corner of the school buildings and, I am sure, reaching the farmhouses a mile away across the valley. Not that anybody turned a hair when this happened, for Trish was looked upon as a local 'character' and accepted as such, booming voice and all.

Whenever I go back to St David's my thoughts inevitably return to Trish, the champion of rebels and dissidents, and the one adult in my young life who was able to accept me as the volatile, social misfit that I was. In their positions at the school my parents were conscious of the need to set high standards of behaviour and appearances, and this naturally spilled over into their expectations of their own children. Being a born maverick, I found these constraints irksome and kicked against the traces continually. The habit has stayed with me to the present day, although I now find that my family are beginning to accept me as I am, even if they are not always able to approve of my behaviour and way of life.

When I was eighteen, and still had no clear idea of what I wanted to do for a living, I went to study art in York. It was while doing my foundation year there that I learned that Trish was dying from cancer. I was devastated by the news and returned to St David's to see her just before she died. As soon as I arrived, I rushed into her bedroom and flung my arms around her neck to give her a bear hug and to tell her how much I loved her. In doing so I clumsily knocked her cancerous leg, causing terrible agony. It was the first, and last, time I ever saw Trish cry, and the memory of my carelessness comes back to haunt me still whenever I think of her.

I was more upset than I could ever have believed possible when Trish died, but it is only now, looking back, that I realize the effect this event had on me, knocking me off-balance and affecting everything I did over the following seven or eight years. She had always been my mainstay and prop, somebody outside the family to whom I could turn in times of trouble, who understood me and loved me, whatever my failings. Now she was dead and everything had gone to pieces; I had no idea which way to turn, and it was to be several chaotic years before I could begin to get myself back on an even keel once again.

Trish, who was only forty-nine when she died, was buried in the little churchyard at Llanrhos near the school entrance. At her funeral the church was filled with mourners, and afterwards everybody went to the funeral tea at Betws yn Rhos. I remember my enormous confusion and anger as I watched people eating as though nothing had happened, nothing had changed — it was my first funeral, and I seemed to have got it all wrong. I cried continuously and was quite unconsolable, to the embarrassment of those around me who kept saying: 'Trish wouldn't have wanted to see you like this' or 'Do be quiet, you are making a fool of yourself.' Last year I went to the funeral of my friend Susie and I cried for her too, but with no inhibitions this time. After all, if you are not able to cry at a funeral, when can you cry?

The old boys of the school clubbed together to fund the memorial to Trish which still stands just outside the door to the main school building — it consists of a renovated cannon (a true relic of the Spanish Armada after it had been blown off-course round the Welsh coast) mounted on a solid wooden base and bearing a brass plaque to Trish's memory. Every time I see this fitting tribute, I once again hear Trish's voice echoing over the playing fields, probably within the same decibel range of a cannon when it is fired, and remember her unforgettable personality with pleasure and affection.

2
FARMER'S WIFE

The first sheepdogs in my life were those I met on farm holidays with the family and, later, on the Llandudno farms where I spent my free time. These dogs made little impression on me — none of them were properly trained and their work with sheep was of the most basic kind, consisting almost solely of an ability to fetch the sheep to the handler some of the time. If more skilled manoeuvres were required, the farmers would begin to shout at the dogs. Then they became confused and would run back home to hide, leaving the sheep to be moved around by the farmer, family and other helpers — a long drawn-out and exhausting procedure. In those days, I took this lack of skill on the part of dog and handler as a fact of life; now that I know better, it makes me sad to think of those poor dogs, under-trained, under-utilized and at the receiving end of abuse and a lack of understanding of their basic needs and true potential.

I was in my teens when I met Tim, Uncle Dan's tri-coloured sheepdog, and first began to appreciate some of the special qualities of his breed. Uncle Dan and Aunt Pat were the parents of my schoolfriend Tina, and I used to go to stay on their farm at St Asaph in North Wales, where Ti, who was also mad on riding, had a big horse called Giles. I had Shane at that time, and friends of my parents would bring him to the farm for me in their horsebox so that Ti and I could attend pony club events together during the holiday, which we did with gusto and enjoyment.

Ti and I already had an interest in the opposite sex and were at the stage where we read all the women's magazines, avidly scanning the problem pages — though with little understanding — and gleaning a lot of useless information including the fact that mudpacks were beneficial to female skin. We had plenty of mud available down by the river and, having assumed that mud was mud was mud, we spent some time daubing our faces and letting it dry to ensure spot-free skin. My aunt Pat was used to the pair of us coming in all mud-spattered after our various energetic activities on the farm, but was a bit taken aback when we started appearing with thick, dried mud caked over our faces!

Each day, when I had finished riding and helping out at the farm, I managed to spend a lot of time with Tim, who was always friendly and affectionate. He was generous, too. Dan's brother, Dewi, ran the slaughterhouse at St Asaph, so Dan used to be given a lot of sheep's heads to feed to the dogs. Tim would bring me his collection of well-gnawed heads one after another, drop them at my feet and then sit down in front of me as though saying, 'Come on, eat the lovely dinner I've brought you.' I always declined the offer, but Tim never took offence and we would sit quietly together amongst the heap of smelly bones. For some reason I have no memories whatever of dogs being worked much on Uncle Dan's farm, but I suppose they must have been used with the flocks at times.

I was about thirteen when I went to stay with Ti and confided in her that a boy had kissed me (it was my first time) and I thought I was pregnant. We both spent a tense and anxious week because I said I could never go home to cause my parents all that worry, so where was I to go? And what would I do with the baby when it arrived? It seems strange to me now, after all my time with animals and learning their mating habits at a very young age, that I had not been able to apply my knowledge to the human situation and get the whole thing better sussed out by that time. It gave me such a fright that it put me off the idea of having children forever, although it has done nothing to stop me from enjoying the company of other people's offspring from time to time.

I have always envied those born into a farming life, the closeness of their family relationships and the seemingly endless fund of knowledge they have about everything to do with farming and the countryside. Not having had the advantage of being from country stock, I have found there is much to learn. I am still striving to catch up with other people in the shepherding world who have been brought up to the task since their earliest days, and along the way I have discovered the invariable kindness of these hard-working people who have included me in their lives. They have always been patient and unstinting in their teaching and in providing answers to my incessant questions.

Cock pheasant

It is probably my lack of a farming background which led to my mixed feelings about shooting. With my love of animals being so pronounced as a child, I felt very protective towards the wildlife around me. That included the pheasants which became so tame that they would move around on our lawn to peck at the breadcrumbs we put out for them, taking no notice of us as we walked about. When the sun caught the cock pheasants' feathers I was fascinated by their iridescent colours

21

and proud bearing, and felt that they were far too beautiful to end up as somebody's dinner. After all, the rare golden pheasants and the occasional white variety were never shot, so why should the more colourful ones be preyed upon? Trish used to annoy me because she never had any qualms about murdering pheasants. If she spotted one on the drive she would aim her car straight at it, put her foot down and charge towards her unsuspecting quarry with single-mindedness and determination. Occasionally she missed, but most of the time she was successful and would carry the dead bird in to give to the school cook, who would dress and cook it after the corpse had been hung for a few days.

Gloddaeth Hall and the land on which it stands is leased from Lord Mostyn, who also owns the surrounding estate, so the whole area is keepered and there are organized shoots in the game season – a time when I would go into action in attempts to save the pheasants. On the morning of a shoot I would get up early, mount my pony and then go galloping over the fields and through the woods, shouting at the pheasants to fly away from danger. Then I would end up in tears when I left to go to school, only to see the Range Rovers coming up the drive, bearing personalized number plates and the hated shooting party.

To make matters worse, Mum would hang dead pheasants in the utility room where the sight of them always sickened me. Then she would serve up roast pheasant for dinner, always some time after the shoot because the birds had to hang for a week or so before they were considered suitable for cooking – something to do with texture and flavour. I would refuse to eat them because I knew where they had come from. The more I thought about eating animals, the less I liked the idea. This led me to refuse to eat meat for a time, although I now have this aspect of life slotted and am able to eat farmed meat – this includes game such as grouse and quail, but I still avoid pheasant and, now that I own a small flock of ducks, I avoid eating duck too! Another food problem I have is that I am unable to eat lamb in the lambing season, although I can enjoy it later in the year.

Nowadays when I see Mr Groome, the gamekeeper at Gloddaeth Hall, he never fails to remind me of the time I was the bane of his life, riding over forbidden territory and frightening all his carefully reared pheasants.

In retrospect, I sometimes think it was a miracle I was never lynched for some of my escapades in those days; the fact that I was not says much for the forbearance and understanding of those I abused.

Fox

Oddly enough, although I enjoy seeing foxes roaming the countryside, I have no reservations about hunting – probably because I went on pony club hunts as a child – and I have to admit I find a certain beauty in the red coat of the huntsman, the sleek, well cared-for horses and the handsome hounds with their continually waving tails. At some of the northern meets they also have little hunting terriers which run with the pack; and, on the fells in Cumbria and in the Dales where horses would never be able to get up and down the steep, rocky slopes, there is also a lot of hunting on foot with hounds and terriers. In the area where I live now there is the Lunesdale Hunt, a foot hunt based just over the border in Cumbria, with which Dick and John Fawcett and Jack, the cow man, hunt; we also have the local pack of Wensleydale Fox Hounds, with about fifteen couple of hounds and eight to ten Lakeland terriers under the Master of Hounds, Maurice Bell of Duerley Farm. If the animal rights people get their way all these animals, including some of the horses, will have to be put down because they will be redundant — and what is more cruel than that?

It is essential to keep the number of foxes down to an acceptable level, and anybody who has seen the carcasses of tiny lambs with their heads bitten off or their entrails hanging out must surely agree with this. In general the hunt only takes out the old, infirm or less intelligent foxes, leaving many of the strongest and healthiest to keep the population going. The sad thing is that, if they are not to be culled by the hunt, foxes will probably be gassed or shot by farmers who previously left them for the hunt to deal with — this type of control will eliminate not just one fox but whole families, many of whom will die a terrible, often lingering death. At least the kill is clean and quick at the end of the hunt, and I know which method I prefer.

Of course, not all hunting with hounds is done with the intention of killing foxes. Hound trailing has been a well-established pastime in the North of England since the 1920s; events are organized by the Hound Trail Association, covering Lancashire and the Lake District, and the Border Hound Trail Association which covers events north of Penrith. In contrast to hunting with hounds, which always take place in the winter months, the hound trailing season runs from the beginning of April to the end of October. Rivalry and excitement are intense amongst the hundreds of competitors and specatators at each race.

Before the hounds are released, two men lay a ten-mile trail by dragging aniseed and paraffin-soaked rags along the ground over the entire route, which consists mostly of rough, difficult terrain. Many of the competitors who race their hounds in this sport keep three or four, often of different ages, and there can be from ten to sixty dogs in any one race, with different classes for pups, adult dogs and old dogs. The hounds are not fed until the end of their race; after all the excitement and hollering of the owners as they cheer their dogs on at the finishing line, each ravenous dog buries its head into its feed bucket, not coming up for air until the meal is finished. Competitors

24

End of the hound trail

can win up to £100 in prize money and there are usually six prizes in all. But I am sure that hound trailing could continue without any prizes at all because the opportunity to test the ability of their hounds, and the sheer adrenalin-producing excitement of it all, are quite enough for the farming people and country lovers who support it.

An ability to drive a tractor is an invaluable asset in farm work, and back in Wales it was my friend Mr Blackberry (my name for Mr Bradbury, the school gardener) who initiated me into this art. He claims that the old Ferguson on which I learned was never the same again — but I doubt if I did it much harm, because it is still in working order. These days Mr Blackberry, puffing away at his pipe, looks exactly the same to me as he did all those years ago, with his balding head, big moustache, woollen sweater and shapeless old tweed trousers over big, mud-spattered boots. He was always accompanied by a yellow Labrador, and when he and the dog went back to the potting shed to 'brew up' I would go down there to join them, holding a steaming mug between my hands while we talked.

I found I could tell Mr Blackberry all my troubles and he would help me to get things sorted out in my mind. He never showed impatience at a mixed-up youngster making demands on his time, even when he discovered that I was putting my pony out after dark to graze on the short, lush grass of his carefully tended rugby pitch. I would creep out at dawn to put the pony back in his own, almost grassless paddock before anybody could see him on forbidden ground, forgetting that ponies leave heaps of their dung to let people know where they have been. The games master and Mr Blackberry eventually complained to my father after a rugby game in which the boys in the scrum were getting covered in horse manure, and I was in trouble yet again. But it was not long before I was once more in the potting shed with my friend and we were pulling up our sleeves to see who had the brownest arms – a routine we still go through to this day whenever we meet.

Before I left school at eighteen I had to do a six-week session of work experience, so I found myself a temporary job at Colwyn Bay Zoo which is just a few miles along the coast from Llandudno. I travelled to the zoo each day on my bike, and was always there early because I was in my element with all those animals around me. I spent most of the time there looking after the children's zoo, which I really enjoyed, particularly the little family of Vietnamese pot-bellied pigs which were delightful companions, full of fun and mischief and very affectionate – the children were fascinated by them, and so was I. Sadly, somebody gave the pigs the wrong feed on one of my days off and they all died in spite of frantic attempts to save them.

I was so upset to see my favourite zoo animals die because of somebody's carelessness that it taught me to take as much care in the preparation of animals' food as I would for my own. As a result I have never yet made a mistake of that kind myself with my own animals, although I must admit to doing something similar to one of my own species. I had been married to my second husband, Jim, for some weeks when I decided to make him a shepherd's pie for dinner. I took the mince out of the refrigerator and prepared the meal with loving care and attention; the result was a tasty shepherd's pie and my new husband's approval. But to my horror Jim was soon struck down with food poisoning, and it was only when he was recovering that I discovered I had inadvertently used some pet mince for the pie. That was the first and last shepherd's pie I ever made!

Each week, a van arrived at the children's zoo with a fresh supply of day-old chicks which were then kept on trays under a lamp, carefully fed, and gazed at by our young visitors who were ignorant of the fact that a number of these fluffy, chirping little babies had to be killed each day and then fed to the small mammals. This was supposed to be my job, but the thought of committing wholesale slaughter of this kind made me feel so sick that I knew I would have to find a way round the problem. That was when I came to an arrangement with the primate keeper — I would clean out the baboon house for him each day if he would kill the chickens for me. He accepted the exchange with alacrity, and I soon learned the reason why — the waste products of baboons are just about the most evil-smelling in the world and their housing, even when done every day, is the most revolting thing I have ever had to clean out. However, I gritted my teeth and got on with the job because the alternative was even less attractive.

Baboons are vicious animals, so before I could clean them out I had to wait until they had gone into the outdoor pen. Then I would close the partition door and get on with the job, with all those baboons hanging on to the wooden partitions and peering in through the glass to scream and shout at me. I spent most of my time in there praying that the glass would remain intact under their onslaught; then, when I had finished, I would stick my tongue out at them with relief before retreating to safety. At least I now know that after doing that job I could clean out anything, so that is one of life's little bonuses.

All the animals at the zoo were well cared for, and I was impressed with the quality of the food given to them. The fruit was always in perfect condition, and when it arrived I would treat myself to a snack to stave off the hunger pangs. That was when I discovered that bananas, chewed with a handful of parrot seed (sunflower seeds), make a tasty and satisfying meal. The animals never seemed to mind sharing their food. What my mother would have said if she had known is a different matter — I am sure that she would have found it difficult to understand why I preferred a zoo diet to her delicious roast pheasant. She certainly objected to the zoo smells clinging to my person when I returned home, and I was never allowed in the house until I had removed my clothes in the garage, put on an old dressing gown and gone upstairs to have a bath in disinfectant.

otter

When my own work in the children's zoo was finished, I was always willing to help out around the place with any jobs which would keep me near the animals. That was how I came to be painting the rail which stood between the public and the puma's cage. I was so engrossed in what I was doing that I backed too near to the cage, and the next thing I knew I was being held back against the bars by huge, hairy paws with a strength which was absolutely terrifying. Fortunately I was wearing a padded jacket, and when I eventually recovered my wits I was able to slip my arms out of the sleeves and get away. I doubt if the boss ever knew about my mishap and I never breathed a word, although nobody could understand afterwards how my badly mauled jacket came to be inside the puma's cage. That was a smart lesson learnt which I will never forget.

It was while I was working in Colwyn Bay that ideas were beginning to crystallize in my mind as to how I wanted to spend my future. I was in no doubt that animals must feature largely in whatever I decided to do, and various ideas began to present themselves. I could work with horses, look after animals at the zoo, become a farm worker, train as a veterinary nurse. All these possibilities were going through my mind, but when it came to actually training for something permanent I found that I either did not have the right academic qualifications or could find no suitable work. I had half-heartedly applied to study at art college, never thinking that I would be offered a place, so when the acceptance letter came from York it began to seem like a good idea. My parents were both encouraging, and Dad told me that God had given me an artistic gift. So, having no alternative involving animals at that time, I went off to college. I soon realized that I had made a terrible mistake although the tutors there, discovering that I was unhappy, did their best to help me to develop my skills. But my heart was never in it, and it was during this time that I began to firm up on the idea that I would like to be a shepherdess.

When I gave up my art studies, shortly after Trish's death, I found myself at a loose end with no clear sense of direction despite the shepherdess idea, and I felt aimless, unhappy and discontented. I had returned to Llandudno and found myself a steady boyfriend, Amos. For once my parents approved of my choice, which was a refreshing change, but there were no animals in my life and I sorely missed their company and the pleasure of looking after them. Before leaving home the year before I had given Eeyore to Ray Beech, one of the teachers at St David's, who had a small farm across the valley, and my pony, Hannibal Hayes, had been sold to somebody on Anglesey. I could find no permanent jobs in farm work and was still casting around for something to do when Dad showed me some information about Camp America, a large organization which runs children's holiday camps in different parts of the United States. I decided that I would spend the summer working there before planning my future.

Camp Four Winds was situated on the Maine coast, and I was appointed to take charge of the arts and crafts teaching there. All the children and staff took part in a full outdoor pursuits programme which I enjoyed as much as the children, but I felt very sorry for some of those youngsters. Most of them were at boarding school in termtime, and were then sent away from home again during the months when they could have been spending time with their families; many of the children were longing for the love and affection they were missing, and their plight only seemed to add to my own growing feelings of frustration and despair. But despite my general unhappiness and restlessness throughout that summer, I was able to immerse myself in the activities at the camp. I enjoyed the experience it gave me, and the busy life I was leading left me with little time to think about my own problems, which were shelved fairly successfully throughout that summer.

While I was there, another member of staff and I used to go out running together to keep ourselves fit. One day we set out in our shorts and tee-shirts as usual, and were steadily running along an empty country road, enjoying the peace and quiet of the countryside, when we suddenly became conscious of an animal's hooves thundering along the tarmac behind us. When we turned round, we saw this huge ram bearing down on us. His head, which had the largest horns I have ever seen on a sheep, was lowered, and I later swore that there was smoke coming from his nostrils. There was no doubt at all about the target for which he was aiming — neither was there any doubt as to his intentions when he caught up with us. So we both shot up trees at the side of the road and sat there, breathless with the exertion, waiting for the ram to go away. But our would-be assailant had no intention of letting us off lightly and he stood there, pawing the ground and snorting, his whole body full of evil intent as we remained glued to our respective perches. About an hour later the ram was still circling the tree when a large estate car slowed to a stop and we heaved a sigh of relief, sure that rescue was imminent. We were wrong.

A man stuck his head out of the car window, looked morosely up at us and said, 'That's the same durned ram which has terrorized me and my family for the past few days. We've had a holiday cabin up in the forest, and the first week was fine. Then this durned animal turned up and we've been unable to leave the cabin ever since — as soon as I put a foot out the door, it ran at me and I had to retreat again. Ruined our holiday. So we're heading for home while we've got the chance.' He started up the engine again and our hearts sank. 'Sorry, can't git out the car in case he recognizes me and goes for me agin.' And he was gone. We were left speechless, and it was only when people came to look for us, after realizing that we were missing, that the ram eventually moved away and we could return to the camp.

After my return from America, my future seemed assured when Amos and I decided to get married. The next few months were busy ones, preparing for the wedding and reception, which was held in the beautiful fifteenth-century entrance hall at St David's. The place was full of guests, family and school staff, with all the trimmings of a traditional middle-class wedding and trumpeters in the minstrels' gallery. I was only nineteen and in love with the idea of marrying a farmer. But I was still fickle and restless, very immature and without the slightest notion of the responsibilities and commitment involved in a long-term relationship. Despite its auspicious beginnings, the marriage was doomed from the start.

My parents were delighted with the match. They were very fond of Amos and got on well with his parents, who were also so pleased that they gave us the Anglesey farm (which Amos was already managing) as a wedding present and, with it, the opportunity for me to become involved with animals again. They even had the farmhouse renovated for us to move into after we married — it was such a marvellous gift that I have always regretted I was never able to repay their thoughtfulness and kindness by making their son happy and presenting them with the grandchildren that they and my parents would have liked.

As time went on at the farm in Anglesey, small sadnesses seemed to add up. They probably took on more significance than they would otherwise have done if I had continued to be happy in my relationship with Amos. I had a strong sense of failure because I had packed in my art course; and, with hindsight, I realize that I was still grieving deeply over Trish's death, which had left me with an intolerable feeling of loss that I was unable to shake off.

During those early months, Amos and I seemed to get on well together. We were both happy and very busy building up the farm, going together to buy our first ewes from the annual Welsh half-bred sale on the mainland of Wales in Ruthin. Our first lambing was hectic, because neither of us knew anything about sheep. But we learned rapidly as we went through the seasons, doing our best to keep mistakes to a minimum, reading round the subject and getting help from local farmers.

Still indelibly imprinted on my memory is the day when I was carrying a lamb out of the barn; its feet were hanging down and one of them became trapped between my legs. I was moving so fast that I had broken the lamb's leg before I could stop the momentum and only realized what I had done when I put the lamb down, only to see her back leg dangling uselessly as she tried to reach her mother to suckle. I was in tears and filled with remorse, but we took the lamb to the vet who applied a plaster to the leg. She was soon on her feet again, and I could then get on with my work with a lighter heart. But I have never forgotten that lamb and doubt if I ever will, for that accident taught me a sharp lesson which is with me still whenever I carry lambs around — something I now do with the utmost care.

During that first lambing season, I also had a little orphan ram lamb which I named Moose. Moose had a box in the kitchen where it was warm, and I would get up every two hours in the night to feed him with milk, using a baby bottle and teat. I watched him grow and he began to follow me about everywhere — until the day when he just keeled over and died. It turned out that I had been overfeeding my lamb and had eventually killed him with kindness, which made me feel dreadful and once more full of guilt — a feeling which seemed to be an almost permanent accompaniment to my everyday life at that time.

I was on the Anglesey farm for my twenty-first birthday. Now that we had plenty of land, my present from my parents was a horse called Charlie. I was delighted to be able to get back to riding, doing all the chores which make a horse's life more comfortable. I mucked out his stable every day, covering the floor with plenty of straw to make him a soft bed; I cleaned the tack until it gleamed, and groomed Charlie till he shone. Then I started to go round on my horse with a basketful of eggs at each side of the saddle, selling them to the local people. I would charge a good price to anybody I thought was comfortably off, but much less to those who seemed hard up. It was not a practical way to do business, I suppose, but I ended up with a fair return on my eggs so the system worked satisfactorily as far as I was concerned.

The horse and I seemed to be getting on well together for a few weeks, but then he began to buck and rear for no apparent reason. He seemed well enough in himself but, try as I might, I was unable to stop what appeared to be just a bad habit. Reluctantly, I eventually took him to the local auction and sold him. I later learned that he had had a kidney infection which was causing the problem, and as soon as this was treated the bucking stopped. Once again I felt remorse, and since that time I have always consulted a vet if an animal begins to behave abnormally.

After I sold Charlie I missed equine company, so I exchanged my saddle for a little Shetland pony who became a great pet, and it gave me hours of pleasure just to watch him enjoying his life on the farm. After acquiring the pony at Llangefni Mart I had no transport to get him home, so I set out to lead him on foot — a distance of several miles. To my surprise, the local sausage man drew up in his little van and said, 'Hop in, the pair of you, and I'll take you home.' After a bit of a struggle to get the pony into the van, we travelled home in style surrounded by the smell of sausages and relieved to be able to do the journey in comfort. Goodness knows what the food inspectors would have said, had they known!

There is no doubt that my farming knowledge increased rapidly during the time I was in Anglesey with Amos. Never having worked full-time on the land before, I found myself for the first time faced with the fact that, as one old farmer put it to me once, 'Where there is life, there is death', and I found it a bitter pill to swallow. In other words, I was coming up against the true realities of farming life and having to adjust to the harshness inherent in that sort of undertaking.

Another thing which Amos and I came up against was occasional unpleasantness from one of our neighbours. We had met with so much help and kindness from the farmers and shepherds on Anglesey that we were taken aback by the attitude of an old farmer whose land adjoined our farm. With stock farming it is very important to keep fences in good repair to prevent animals from straying, and where there is a shared fence there are clear rules as to which farmer holds the responsibility for its upkeep. Mr Hughes was responsible for one of the shared fences but would never repair it properly, always doing a botched job. As a result our sheep would get out and wander on to his field. When we approached him about the problem he refused to repair the fence, threatening to put our sheep out on to the road if they strayed again — which they did, of course, because the fence was still broken. We eventually found our sheep, but many of them had strayed several miles along the Anglesey roads and some had been killed by traffic in the process. We were both exhausted by the time we got them home and into another field, and I lost my temper completely. I went off to Mr Hughes's place to have a word with him, and he made me so angry that I ended up by punching him on the nose. I was reported to the police for assault, although the matter never went any further than that; but I have have always felt that my action that day was well deserved.

A further problem for me was that, having married a pleasant young farmer and moved into a lovely farmhouse surrounded by green, fertile land full of animals which I loved, I had achieved a lifelong ambition and therefore found it difficult to understand why my unhappiness was increasing. Trish was gone, so I was no longer able to turn to her for advice. Although my parents tried to help me by saying, 'Everybody has to make adjustments when they are first married – you have to work at even the best relationships', the situation just grew steadily worse. I was completely happy when working on the farm, but soon found that I was not cut out for married life. I rebelled at the restrictions it imposed on my freedom and personal time, and generally behaved in a negative, selfish and immature fashion. In the end the only solution seemed to be to leave Amos, but it was a decision I did not make lightly for I knew that I would hurt not only him but also family and friends. In addition, I had no idea what I was going to do or where I would go when I left – I was once more in limbo, completely confused and very unhappy. I finally left Amos just over a year after we married. Although I have never regretted my decision I still have feelings of sadness and guilt about that time in my life, and can only hope that increased maturity and understanding of myself will enable me to come to terms with it all one day.

3
BESOTTED WITH SHEEPDOGS

I t was during my marriage to Amos that I went to my first sheepdog trial at Benllech on Anglesey, little realizing the effect it was to have on me. Amos and I were having great difficulty in working properly with our flock of a hundred and fifty Welsh half-breds, and it was beginning to dawn on us that a trained dog would save us a lot of work if we could find the right one. When I first arrived at the trial I was only mildly curious to see what the dogs could do, but by the end of the day I was so impressed with the rapport between the handlers and their dogs, with the controlled way the dogs worked with sheep, and with the quiet authority of the farmers and shepherds who were competing, that I made a resolution. One day, come what may, I would be out there competing with them. During the journey home in the old Land Rover I was busy planning how I would achieve this new aim, and I was filled with an enthusiasm which has remained with me, undiminished, ever since.

Amos bought a sheepdog pup named Bill, who turned out to be a good dog on sheep, with a natural instinct for the work. He needed very little training and proved to be a useful dog around the farm, saving us a lot of time and energy. Some time later I acquired a dog pup which had been sired by Bill — the one I called Sykes, after his bulldog namesake. That was my first foray into the sheepdog world, but, as I had never trained a sheepdog before, I soon understood that I would need some help and began to look for ways of getting it. That was when I contacted the Agricultural Training Board (ATB) and began to attend the sheepdog training courses held each week by Emlyn Roberts, a sheepdog handler who farmed at Rhos y Bol on Anglesey and competed at trials in his spare time.

When I started training Sykes, I decided to get a few sheep of my own. At the Anglesey Show I had fallen in love with some Poll Dorset sheep, so I bought three pedigree ewes of this breed from a farmer in Caernarfon and took them home with me, full of plans about the magnificent pedigree flock I would build up in the future from this foundation stock. At this time Amos and I were getting a lot of help from Gareth Evans of the Agricultural Development Advisory Service (ADAS); he was a first-class man with sheep and it was an education to watch him handle them in all situations, always quiet, deliberate and unruffled. He would sit with me for hours, talking to me about sheep and answering my questions, and I can see him now, looking rather like an old Herdwick ram. He used to go on about sheep's teeth and the fact that they must have a good mouth if they were to keep sound. This always amused me because he himself had the worst teeth I had ever seen — just two or three dotted about his mouth — but he seemed to be in pretty good nick otherwise.

The Poll Dorset sheep proved to be more docile than the Welsh half-bred flock we had on the farm, and were ideal to use for training the dogs. I only wished that my dog could be as docile as the sheep, but that was a vain hope in the circumstances. Success with my sheepdog eluded me at that time, but at least I won a prize at the Royal Welsh Show a couple of years later with a home-bred Poll Dorset ewe lamb — I knew she was less than perfect and had gone slightly lame, but I showed her none the less and she won second prize. Whether the fact that I was wearing a bikini in the show ring, in response to a friend's dare, swayed the judges' thinking I will never know; it could have been the heat, but I have my suspicions! Horace, the aged Dorset ram which I had also taken to the show, never got as far as the ring — for once I took the advice of those who knew better when they told me that, with only one horn, one eye permanently half-closed and marriage tackle which trailed along the ground, he was a most unlovely specimen. So I had to be satisfied with my ewe's second place, and returned home well pleased with myself.

Every day, when the farm work was finished, I took Sykes out to the sheep and worked very hard with him in efforts to turn him into a good working dog. I continued to attend Emlyn's training classes each week, and was so honed in on the idea of training the dog that I gave no thought to the idea of training myself at the same time. I had grown passionate in my desire to become a competent sheepdog handler, but the combination of my impulsive, noisy and often brash personality, and Sykes's lack of a true herding instinct, was to prove lethal to our joint efforts. However, it was to be a couple of years before I was prepared to admit myself beaten and call it a day.

When Sykes and I won the little ATB sheepdog trial held at the end of one of Emlyn's courses I basked in the approbation of the other students, and my confidence grew out of all proportion to my modest achievement. However, I was soon brought down to size again. I began to compete at small local sheepdog trials, where Sykes proved to be so useless that I would end up by raising my voice and shouting at him as he disappeared into the distance. On the odd occasions when he did manage to find his bunch of sheep, my dog would take them round the field at such a lick that the sheep became quite unstoppable and the run would end in total disorder. The other handlers pulled my leg unmercifully. The veteran trainer and handler H. Glyn Jones and his wife, Beryl, have told me that the first time they saw me at a trial I was wearing bright red overalls and was down on my knees begging my dog to do as I asked him. Speak to anybody in the Welsh trialling scene today, and I guarantee that they would all remember Sykes and this newcomer of a handler who never had a clue what she was doing but did it with great concentration, noise and enthusiasm!

Without knowing it, I was beginning to meet some of the best sheepdog handlers in the British Isles as I went the rounds of local trials and eventually began to compete on the North Wales mainland. It was some time later before I learned that Glyn was a previous International Supreme Championship winner in 1973, had been the Welsh National Champion two years running in 1980 and 1981 with Bwlch Taff, and had innumerable other successes to his credit. Then there was Meirion

H. Glyn Jones' Taff

Jones, who has twice won the International Supreme Championship, in 1959 and 1988, as well as the Welsh National Championship in 1979, and has had over two thousand other open trial wins. John Lightfoot later won the Welsh National Championship, in 1991, while Gwyn Jones was International Supreme Champion in 1974, 1976 and 1990, and had the 1987 Welsh National Championship to his credit. And there were many others, including the legendary Alan Jones and E. Wyn Edwards, both previous winners at national and international level. So I was competing in illustrious company, and once I appreciated this I sensibly and gratefully picked their brains at every opportunity. As

I crept off the field each time after another disastrous run with Sykes, John Lightfoot would greet me with words of cheer and a barley sugar, saying, 'I reckon you'll need this to soothe your throat.' Even though I have learnt to discipline myself to be quiet in my dog handling now, John still hands me a barley sugar, saying, 'Just in case.'

In those early days, Glyn Jones was probably the person from whom I learned the most about training sheepdogs. I eventually became very friendly with him and Beryl and their daughter, Ceri, who is also a successful sheepdog trainer and handler in her own right. Ceri and I have always enjoyed each other's company; we are both very independent people, we are women in a man's world when we compete at trials, we have a shared interest in the dogs — but completely different personalities. The amalgam seems to work well. I still visit the family whenever I am near their North Wales farm, avidly listening to Glyn's pearls of wisdom about dogs and enjoying his anecdotes which seem to be endless, for he is a great personality with a prodigious memory of times past. The trouble was that, when I started out on this sheepdog training lark, I consistently ignored the best bit of advice Glyn ever gave me: 'You're wasting your time with that dog. You should sell him and buy a couple of youngsters from registered working stock — I guarantee you'll have more success if you do that.' But I kept putting off the evil day.

The one thing in which I managed to train Sykes really well was the 'stop' command: he would stop on a sixpence any time I whistled, whatever he was doing. But I failed to teach him much else. He had no natural feel for sheep and would barge about the field with his head in the air and no 'eye' at all — and it is the eyes, in conjunction with his body position, which a dog uses to control his sheep. My inexperience, of course, did nothing to help either. After I had set Sykes off at a trial, it would not be long before I was shouting and yelling at the dog, my agitation making him even more excited and irrational and probably wrecking any innate ability he might have had. At this time, I only had one whistle command for my dog (the stop whistle), which I achieved by placing two fingers in my mouth in the time-honoured way. All the other commands were voice only, which is one of the reasons I would end up shouting my head off. I tried to use the traditional flat shepherd's whistle but with singular lack of success, although I did master this essential art a few years later when

I was with my second husband. Now I wonder how I could ever have managed without it.

Meirion Jones spent time with me after my runs, giving me a lot of good advice, although things continued to go askew because I lacked experience, was very nervous and, as a result, tended to rush things. Meirion had noticed this and, before my run at the Henryd trial near Conway, he suggested that I should try counting up to ten after Sykes had stopped at the end of his outrun from me to the far side of the sheep. Only then should I ask him to lift his sheep — to make contact with them for the first time.

The time for my run arrived and I walked out to the post with Sykes, confident that this time I would do better. Sykes's outrun was perfect, and he stopped behind his sheep at the top of the field the minute I gave him the command to do so. The trouble was that, by the time I had counted up to ten, the sheep had come running down the field on their own. They galloped past me as I stood watching them in horror, and then rushed straight into the refreshment tent where they created havoc. All this time Sykes was lying at the top of the field, as good as gold, waiting for me to give him the command to bring the sheep to me. After I had caught the sheep (with a little help from my friends and their dogs) I went over to Meirion, who was his usual laconic self. 'Try counting to four next time,' was all he said.

When I left Amos I took with me my nanny goat, Horlicks, and Gandhi the gander (with his harem of geese), and went to live in a caravan which I christened 'Shepherd's Pie'. It stood in a field on Emlyn's farm, where I looked after ten sows and helped Emlyn and his father, John, with the sheep. All the rest of my time I spent training Sykes and competing at sheepdog trials.

I loved the pigs, especially a sow called Mrs Thomas, and I kept a piglet out of her called Porky who, although he was never the brightest of his kind, could round up the sheep much better than Sykes ever did! I remember I gained a certain notoriety in the Llangefni Mart the day I took a Land Rover full of young pigs to be sold in the ring. Being an old vehicle, the catch to its back door was always difficult to fasten; on this day, it gave way. All my lively young charges spilled out in the middle of the town and went racing off in different directions, causing traffic chaos as everything came to a standstill on the busiest day of the week. There is nothing more difficult to catch than a squealing, lively little pig which has suddenly found its freedom, and it was several hours before they were all caught and peace reigned once more. It was a long time before people stopped pulling my leg about the incident and even now, whenever I return to Anglesey, I am still reminded of that day.

Mrs Thomas

Those pigs were very intelligent and lovable animals, reminding me of the little pot-bellied variety at the zoo, so I was always ultra-careful about their food mix and kept a careful watch for any signs of illness. But they thrived, making good mothers to the litters they produced and responding to the affection I gave them as they went about enjoying their lives. To me, there is no finer sight than a family of healthy, happy, busy pigs in their natural surroundings, and I always feel sad when I see the big commercial pig farms, where the sows are kept in tiny pens and restrained from reaching their babies to lick them after birth, or to nuzzle them affectionately. Nor is there any bedding (or room) available for the pregnant sow to satisfy her nesting instincts by making herself a big bed of straw immediately before she farrows down, and this must cause untold distress to these affectionate and normally loving mothers. I am just not interested in that kind of farming – to me it is not farming at all, but an inhumane use of livestock to make money, with no rights for the animals which are simply used like machines. So-called civilization seems to have led us to some peculiar practices.

My pigs' owners, Emlyn and his parents, were very good to me when I was starting off with my dogs, giving me some sound advice and doing everything they could to help. As I was having difficulty in penning sheep, Emlyn would put up hurdles for me and encourage me by shouting 'Great, just like Alan Jones,' when I did occasionally get them in. That was the highest praise in the world to me because Alan, a farmer from a little place called Pontllyfni who is known as one of the all-time greats in the sheepdog world, is one of the best penners in the business. So I would feel really good – until I got it wrong next time. Alan subsequently suffered a long illness, but was still able to carry on farming and trialling with his dogs. I have a vivid memory of him, shortly after he had been discharged from hospital a few years ago, competing at a trial while still on crutches – and winning!

Gradually I began to learn more about the serious task of shepherding, and it was at this time that I learned how to shear a sheep using hand shears – an old art which has largely given way to the faster, electric variety, but gives the shearer much more satisfaction in a job well done. Hand shearing contests are still held at agricultural shows and some sheepdog trials, and it is lovely to watch the shepherds, old and young, sitting on the shearing stool with a ewe in front of them, carrying on the tradition of their forebears in a skilful and unhurried manner.

Indeed in many of the more remote parts of Wensleydale, where there is no electricity, sheep are still routinely sheared by hand. During my first two years in my present job at Richard's Fawcett farm we would all go up to Dodd Fell together at shearing time; three or four of us would be shearing by hand, with a couple using electric shears run off the tractor motor. Then, after Jack injured his back and was unable to shear any more, we began to use a shed with a power supply on a neighbouring farm, so now everybody can use electric shears. But I still plod on with hand shears, which I prefer. I am usually given all the old girls with half their wool hanging off, but I get a lot of pleasure from trimming them up and sending them out looking neat and tidy — and several years younger.

Shearing

But all that lay in the future. Meanwhile, back on Anglesey, a short distance across the fields from my caravan stood the smallholding of Dr Sheila Grew, who taught me a great deal about the general care of sheepdogs and puppies. In her early sixties and crippled with arthritis and angina, Sheila lived alone in an isolated cottage with her ten Border Collies, litters of puppies, bantams in the back garden and a small flock of Llanwenog sheep on her few acres of land. Despite failing health and strength, Sheila tended her smallholding and animals with dedication and affection right to the end of her life and was looked upon as a great character by all who knew her, making some enemies and a lot of friends on the way.

As Sheila was only able to move around with the aid of two sticks, Emlyn and I helped her with her sheep whenever we could — we dosed them, clipped them, treated their feet and took them to market, and she was always very kind to me whenever I went to see her. Nobody could ever say that Sheila was easy to get on with — she had endless patience with her animals, which she loved to distraction, but she did not have the same affection for people in general and made no effort to hide this fact. She reminded me of Trish in many ways — the same square build, abrasive personality, booming voice, tendency to favouritism, sweet tooth and inability to suffer fools gladly. But I got on well with her, and grew to respect and like her.

Sheila was the founder of a small magazine called *Working Sheepdog News* — an achievement of which she was justifiably proud — and all her time indoors was spent in compiling the next issue or dealing with the mountain of administration. Although solitary and cut off in her cottage, with few visitors, she valued the telephone and letter contact she built up through the magazine, and looked upon many of the regular subscribers as her friends, never forgetting a name or the details of their various dogs and achievements. Sheila really slaved over the magazine until it became too much for her, and after seven years' hard work she passed it over to somebody else. When she died, only a couple of sheepdog people attended her funeral. I felt very sad to think that more of them had not made the effort to pay their last respects to a woman who had rendered them such an invaluable service for so many years.

One of Sheila's greatest pleasures was breeding from her bitches. She selected stud dogs with care, going to trials to watch them running, studying their lines and abilities and matching them to the lines of the bitch she was using. It was a joy to watch Sheila as she prepared the dam for whelping — grooming her, feeding her with care, and introducing her to the whelping area two weeks before the pups were due. She fussed around like a mother hen and spent many anxious hours while the bitch was in labour, never relaxing until the pups had all arrived and were suckling from their mother — then Sheila would sit down with a small glass of sherry 'To celebrate'.

I remember going to see her one day after I had learnt that she had a new litter of puppies. But when I dashed into the whelping area to see them, Sheila was absolutely furious with me. At first I was unable to understand why she was so angry, but after calming down she explained about the dangers of carrying infection on my feet, clothing and hands. That was when I learned about the terrible new disease called parvovirus which was then raging throughout the British Isles, decimating the dog population and wiping out whole litters of puppies in a few hours. Sheila went on to explain. 'Even if dogs are protected against other diseases by vaccination, there is still no effective vaccination available against parvovirus. In any case, even if dogs don't develop the disease themselves, they can still excrete the virus in their faeces and you could carry the infection here from your animals. Never, ever do that again with a litter of puppies.' She was practically in tears and I felt terrible, but I learned another lesson that day which I have never forgotten and, fortunately, the puppies were reared without mishap. Some time after this incident, an effective vaccine was produced and parvovirus infection is now well controlled. (More information on parvovirus can be found in Chapter 8.)

As I got to know Sheila better, she would talk to me about her past life and achievements. I found that she had the most remarkable memory, with an enviable ability to recall names and events from years past. Educated in England and Denmark as a child, she had studied medicine at the Royal Free Hospital in London, qualifying as a doctor in 1943. She then worked in general medicine until 1946, when she joined the Save the Children organization as Assistant Medical Officer and worked towards relieving the misery of the thousands of displaced children to be found in Europe at that time. Although Sheila never married (she tended to be rather scathing about men in general) she adopted two sons, Richard and Simon, rearing them single-handed. She worked in various parts of Britain as a general practitioner before becoming County Medical Officer in Gloucestershire and settling there for a number of years.

It was in 1962 that a disaster struck Sheila which was to alter the whole pattern of her life. After successful surgery for breast cancer she was left with a permanent disability in one arm and hand. Despite this, and with the great enthusiasm which was one of her most endearing qualities, Sheila gave up medicine to embark on a new career in farming. She bought Gaerwen Isaf, a farm in South Wales which was to provide her with the prefix of Gaerwen for her line of International Sheepdog Society-registered sheepdogs. In addition to breeding Border Collies Sheila had a flock of a hundred breeding ewes and a herd of Charolais cattle. She learned fast and worked hard, and also branched out into breeding Welsh Cob ponies. In all these undertakings she was successful.

Some years later Sheila's deteriorating health forced her to to give up the farm, but, indomitable as ever and wanting to maintain her interests in dogs and farm animals, she had a succession of smallholdings before moving to her last home in Anglesey. Here she was near her adopted sons, who were both settled in North Wales with their families — and it was here that I first met her.

At a time when most people would have retired gracefully Sheila still threw herself into her various projects with enthusiasm and delight, defying the weather even while her failing body played mayhem with her every movement. She found these physical limitations painful, irksome and frustrating, but she kept that marvellous brain of hers active — always eager to learn and disseminate information, particularly about sheepdogs. In addition to running the magazine, she wrote two books on the forebears of the modern registered Border Collie which have become classics of their kind, and she was working on a third when she died. Sheila lived her life to the full right to the end, when she had a massive coronary and never returned home from hospital. She will always be remembered by people who knew her for her tremendous courage, agile brain, well-developed sense of humour, firmly held opinions and love of argument.

I lived in the caravan for about a year and, despite the kindness of many people, it was a very unhappy time when I was once more riddled with feelings of guilt and inadequacy, with no real sense of direction in my life. But there was a light beginning to show at the end of the tunnel. I had become so besotted with sheepdogs that I had something to concentrate my mind on, and I was at last doing something which I wanted to do and not necessarily something which was expected of me. This sounds very selfish, and probably was. But, rightly or wrongly, I felt at the time that for most of my life I had been trying to — or had been made to — conform to other people's expectations of me. For the first time I was beginning to feel free to be my own person, and the prospect enthralled me. This is probably one of the reasons why I became so single-minded in my determination to succeed in the training of my dogs — all my waking hours, when I was not working, were spent with the dogs either on the fields or at sheepdog trials. I was avid for information, listened to all the advice given me, and read anything I could lay my hands on about training working sheepdogs. But applying my new-found knowledge was a different matter, and I found the going very tough.

Family and friends not connected with the sheepdog world who came to visit me at that time in my life have since told me they were convinced I was going quietly batty. My great pal Ti said that all I could talk about was sheep and dogs. I even refused to go out for a drink when this was suggested, preferring to go down to the field to do some training, or to clean out the dogs' sleeping places. In short, I was boring everybody to death and seemed totally disinterested in my friends' lives and achievements. Ti thought I was growing into a peculiar, pig-headed, uninteresting woman, and it was some years before we got together again and she realized that I had just been going through an odd phase. The passion for dogs and sheep has remained, but there are now many other things in my life to provide a sensible balance, and my friendships have survived in the long term.

My parents also had a bad time with me (the story of our lives). Not only had I left Amos, but I was still unsettled and difficult, quick-tempered, intolerant when given advice, and a general pain in the neck. Neither were matters improved by the language I used when some friends of my parents filmed me training my dogs. This was not a deliberate act on my part — I had not realized that they were recording sound as well. Mum and Dad were very upset when the video was played back on their television and my exasperated expletives came across, loud and clear. But, despite all this, my parents were always there if I needed them and never cut themselves off from me, although I think they had to work very hard at accepting me when I was at my worst. It was some time before I began to understand that, to make that sort of effort, they must have a great affection for me.

While I was in the caravan Emlyn's father, John, gave me a beautiful crook which had been made by Bob Gruff (Robert Gruffydd Jones), a retired shepherd and sheepdog handler who has become well known for his stick making. It had a blackthorn shank and a ram's horn head, with a sheepdog carved on one side and 'Katy' on the other – a real work of art. I treasured this gift, my first real crook, until it was stolen some years later at a sheepdog trial. I have had other crooks since then, but would give a lot to get that first one back again because it meant so much to me.

John also gave me a Border Collie puppy which I named Bonky Bill – and, oh boy, did that dog live up to his name! So now I had two dogs, both turning into poor work dogs and also quite unsuitable for trialling. But, being a supreme optimist (and a foolish one), I pressed on with their training and competed at trials with them, refusing to accept that I should cut my losses and start again. I was making a fundamental mistake – I loved my dogs so much that I was not prepared to stand back from them to enable me to assess them objectively. It was not until I met another famous handler – and fell in love with him – that I was to learn how to do so.

I have always found older men attractive and seem to get on well with them, and Jim Cropper (who was almost twice my age) was no exception to this when he first caught my eye in 1984 at Bala in Wales – it was the first time I had seen him standing at the post at a sheepdog trial, although I had already heard about his skill with sheepdogs from other handlers who knew him. What really impressed me at that moment was the way Jim was handling his dog. He is a large man with a big voice and a terrific laugh, but he was commanding his dog so quietly that it was sometimes difficult to hear him from the sidelines. Jim's movements were as restrained and calm as his commands, and I noticed that his dog was also quiet and deliberate in his movements, listening carefully for further directions but never taking his eyes off the sheep.

After Jim's run I went over to introduce myself to him, and we stood talking about dogs for a long time and analysing runs as they occurred. I was fascinated by his knowledge and also by the man himself, but we did not meet again until a few weeks later when we were both competing in North Wales at the British Subaru Championship trials in Pwllglas – a trial which has become a firm favourite with competitors. I have competed at this event since it began in 1982, and I think it is one of the best trials in the British Isles now. It is certainly the biggest, with over 370 dogs running in the various classes over two days; so there is plenty of stiff competition, with all the top handlers vying with each other for the honours. I have never been amongst the winners there yet, but I plan to be up there one day.

It was at the 1984 Subaru trial that I first tried to get sponsorship for myself. Everybody told me I was flogging a dead horse because I was not well enough known at that time, but I decided to show them all that they were wrong. So I went over to the Subaru trade stand, spoke to the promotions manager, and told him that I would shortly become famous and was worth sponsoring. As predicted, I got nowhere at all. However some years later, in November 1990, he finally took me up on my suggestion after reading an article in the *Independent* newspaper, which reported that I had rolled up to one of my demonstrations in a beat-up old Subaru. That was when I was presented with my first new pick-up. My name was emblazoned on the side, which took a bit of getting used to, but as the months passed I soon forgot the advertising material as I began to appreciate what a great all-weather, all-terrain vehicle I had been given. It made a grand dogmobile, and there was still more than enough room for an injured ewe or two, a couple of bags of sheep nuts and some bales of hay. With the first heavy fall of snow that winter nobody else could get their vehicles out of the village, but mine did it in style and I was able to get to the sheep with their food after passing other people who were stuck in the snow.

Jim won the Subaru Championship that day in 1984. He was running Lad, a handsome, four-year-old black and white dog. As a hushed crowd watched, it was obvious to everybody that we were witnessing a classic run. Jim was as quiet as ever in his handling, while Lad worked perfectly and paced the sheep exactly right — it was as near to perfection as any run I have ever seen, and the applause at the end was terrific. At this time Lad was coming into his prime and everybody was forecasting that he and Jim would one day win the coveted International Supreme Championship together. But the hand of fate was about to deal a cruel blow which nobody could have anticipated on that victorious summer's day when Lad and Jim went up to be presented with their trophies.

4
ANOTHER BITE AT THE CHERRY

'Lad has injured one of his back legs!' It was shortly after the Subaru trial, and I could tell by the tone of Jim's voice on the other end of the phone that he was very upset. 'The dog went missing, and my son found him as he was walking to the pit this morning. The poor dog was hanging by his back leg from some fencing. He'd been struggling to free himself for some time, but he'd only managed to entangle himself more and more in the barbed wire at the top. He was absolutely exhausted when James managed to unhook him, and then he had to be carried home.'

I was horrified and sympathetic, wondering how bad the injury was. Then Jim dropped his bombshell. 'I took the dog straight to the vet, and he says the leg will have to be amputated.' I stood there in stunned silence. A lump came into my throat as I thought of that beautiful dog and the graceful way he had moved about the trials field only days before. I swallowed hard and my eyes filled with tears.

'I don't think it would be fair to keep the dog,' Jim was saying. 'He'll never be able to run properly again, so I think I'd better have him put down.'

'Oh, you can't do that!' I blurted out, and then went on, 'Lots of farm dogs have lost legs in accidents and they manage to do their work on three legs. At least give him a chance. Then, if it's too much for him, it *would* probably be kinder to have him destroyed. *Please* give it a try, Jim.'

Lad

The outcome was that the leg was amputated and Jim decided to keep the dog to see how things would go, but I suspect it was not my pleading which did the trick. After a very successful trialling career, Jim had given up farming for a while and was working at the local coalmine. As a result, he had cut down on the time he spent competing with his dogs. He had just taken up the sport again seriously when he acquired Lad, and when the dog proved to have exceptional ability Jim began to compete enthusiastically once more. It was likely that he was so fond of the dog he could not bear the thought of putting him down — although I doubt if he would ever admit such a thing.

I was still struggling to train Sykes and Bonky, but getting nowhere; so I wrote to Jim asking him if he could help me to train them. In his reply he told me that I was the one who needed training in how to handle a dog, but that this could not be done at a distance. He suggested that I go up to his home in Lancashire for a series of lessons. So a few days later I found myself travelling up there with Jim, who had come down in his car to collect me and my dogs. I was only supposed to be staying there for a week, but as it turned out I never went back to North Wales.

When I arrived in Rossendale I met all the Cropper family, including the children from Jim's previous marriage, James, Morgan and Linda, who were the same generation as me. Everybody was so curious about the female sheepdog handler they had heard about that they called round to the house to view me, and for a time I felt a bit like a goldfish in a bowl. But they were all very pleasant and friendly and later became good friends. It must have been especially difficult for Linda when I first arrived. Since her parents' divorce when she was about twelve she had stayed with her father, housekeeping for him and looking after his dogs. She had also learnt how to handle sheepdogs, occasionally going to trials with her father and competing with his dog, Fonzi. When I later moved in with Jim she found it difficult to accept me, but as we grew to know each other better our friendship blossomed, based on a shared interest in animals in general, a passion for horses in particular, and a genuine liking for each other.

I had thought my life in the caravan was pretty grim in the cold weather, but it paled into insignificance when compared to Jim's house which was unbelievably spartan and cold. When he showed me my bedroom, I tried to switch on the light. After nothing happened, Jim just laughed and said, 'Nay, lass, there hasn't been a light in there for eighteen years, tha' knows.'

There was no offer to effect repairs to improve my comfort, so I just had to manage the best I could. I have always considered myself to be fairly tough, but that was before I met Jim and discovered that he is impervious to cold, discomfort or inconvenience of any kind. Having a bath in that house was rather like taking one's ablutions in one of those big freezers they use for meat storage — the ones where, if you get locked in, you can freeze to death in about half an hour. I would run the hottest bath possible, climb into it and then spend the next ten minutes gathering up the courage to leap out again into the howling gale blowing in from the window, which was devoid of glass. I always stuffed the hole with towels as soon as I went into the bathroom, but they seemed to make little difference to the general temperature. It is hardly surprising that my teeth would start chattering as I hastily dried myself, before throwing layers of warm clothing on to my still damp, shivering body. After a few days of this I decided that, to be a farmer, you have to be either somebody very special or completely mad, and I came to the conclusion that Jim was the special variety. As I was soon head over heels in love, I eventually moved in with him — at least it was one way of keeping warm — and we married a few months later.

Since I like to see hens around the place, Jim and I went out to buy some and he built me a fine henhouse for them. Both of us enjoyed eating the eggs when the pullets started to lay a little while later. We bought their feed from a local man who recommended old-fashioned corn and oats as the most suitable thing — then we discovered that, if this mixture was soaked overnight and cooked in the morning, it made a delicious porridge for our own breakfast! Although we were always buying and selling dogs, we spent any profits on the petrol to go to trials, on the fees for entering our dogs, and on our social life in the pub, which we both enjoyed. As a result we were always short of money, and economy with the housekeeping was essential. Jim would cook sometimes, his 'flanny' of vegetables, oats, eggs and cheese being my favourite. Jim never tidied up after himself, and I doubt if he ever washed the vegetables before using them — but in spite of this, the results were very tasty.

My own cooking had not improved at all, although I did try to make sense of some of the recipes which looked so good in the cookery books but never seemed to resemble the beautiful colour pictures, even when I did get the ingredients right. The first rhubarb pie I made was too long to go into the oven — I had left the sticks of rhubarb whole since there was nothing in the recipe about chopping them into small pieces. I covered them with sugar and wrapped pastry round them. Then I carefully sealed the edges, brushed the top with milk, sprinkled sugar on it and stood back to admire my handiwork, certain that I had made the ultimate in rhubarb pies. I opened the oven door to put it in — and the pie stuck across the opening. Disaster.

On another occasion we were expecting some people who were bringing their bitch to one of the dogs, so I decided to make some biscuits for them to have with a cup of tea. Everything went smoothly for once, and the biscuits looked really good when I took them out of the oven. But after our visitors had left I found half-eaten biscuits in plant pots, behind cushions and under the saucers. I soon discovered why they had been discarded when I bit into one and almost broke a tooth.

Jim and I had been living together for only a few weeks before the biggest event of the sheepdog trialling year took place at York. I had never attended the International Sheep Dog Trials before, so I was full of excitement as we drove north to spend three days immersed in handlers, sheep and dogs, and watching the country's top competitors vying for the coveted Supreme Championship. From our seats in the grandstand, Jim and I were engrossed in the runs and I felt as though nothing could be more perfect. I was sharing the occasion with a man I had grown to love and who had already competed at this event himself many times in the past, winning the 1973 Brace Championship with his dogs Fleet and Clyde, and just being pipped at the post in the Supreme Championship the same year.

The bush telegraph had been working overtime, and I think everybody we met at that International had heard the news about Jim and me. We were teased unmercifully by friends and enemies alike. By the end of those few days they were to have another incident to add to the fund of tales which seemed to be proliferating about us.

We had returned to our hotel and were in the bar, having a drink with other sheepdog people who were staying there. One wall of the bar was made entirely of glass and overlooked the hotel swimming pool, which was empty and, to my eyes, most inviting. Being a strong swimmer, I always feel that I want to be in water whenever I see it; inevitably I said to Jim: 'I'd love to have a swim.' 'Go on, then,' he replied. So off I marched, down a small corridor to the poolside where, false modesty never having been one of my strong points, I removed my clothes and dived in. Seconds later, Jim had joined me. I can still see the expressions on the faces of all those people lined up on the other side of the glass to watch us enjoying our swim. The following morning when we walked into the grandstand all conversation stopped for a few moments, so people had obviously heard of our escapade the night before. When we returned to our hotel room that night we found that the proprietors had hung a huge picture on the wall above the bed, depicting a whale and a mermaid swimming together!

During the years I spent in Rossendale I became very fond of Jim's mother, Ethel, and we have remained good friends even though I eventually walked out on her son. Ethel is now well into her seventies, but keeps herself active around the little terraced cottage where she lives with Jim's father. She still enjoys going for a night out and a drink at the local, and whenever I am in the area I try to visit her.

Ethel takes a lot of care with her appearance, insisting that nobody sees her in the morning until she has all her make-up on and her hair is done (still jet-black, but whether by nature or man-made I have never dared to enquire). Then she is the most hospitable person I have ever met. When I first visited her, she asked me, 'Dost 'ee fancy a bit o' parkin, lass?' I had no idea what parkin was, but nodded my head; then she served up squares of this lovely, dark brown, sticky, gooey cake which she had made herself. After that, whatever the time of day I arrived, Ethel always insisted on feeding me. 'Ee, lass, it's good to see you. I'll just put a pie in t'oven for you,' and I would leave feeling pounds heavier than when I arrived. I admired and envied her culinary skills, but unfortunately they never rubbed off on to me.

Ethel always does her washing on Mondays, ironing on Tuesdays, baking on Wednesdays, and hates to be disturbed in her weekly routine, which is sacrosanct. She organizes her husband in the same way, and they go to their local pub together on regular evenings out. Some years ago Jim's dad (also named Jim) had a hip operation which went wrong, and he has never been able to sit down since − he either has to stand up or to lie down, so it is hardly surprising that he has ended up by being rather tetchy and grumpy for much of the time. However, in those days he would stand at the bar singing his favourite song, 'Old Shep', and then Ethel would get going with her favourites − 'The Crystal Chandelier' and 'My Coat of Many Colours'. Sadly, old Jim spends most of his time in bed these days, so I doubt if Ethel is able to get out much. But she is never too busy to send me cards for Christmas and my birthday.

Brought up at a time when it was considered wicked to have idle hands, Ethel has always spent her leisure time constructively. For many years now, she has made crocheted rugs and blankets, resulting in neatly folded heaps of these carefully crafted items all over the house. Family and friends refuse to take any more, nor can she sell them, but Ethel still crochets away because she enjoys it.

When I told Ethel that I never wanted children she was very understanding. She said to me once, 'You're not going to nurse, are you?' and it was a few minutes before I realized that she was talking about having a baby. 'No blooming fear,' I answered fervently, and she grinned at me. 'Well, in that case, if you ever think you are, get a bottle of gin and have a very hot bath.' 'Don't worry, Ethel,' I reassured her, and made sure that my supply of pills was to hand all the time under the old pig trough. Babies were not in my scheme of things, either then or at any time in the future.

Of course, my babies at that time were my precious little pedigree Dorset sheep, and I moved them to Lancashire after deciding to stay with Jim. But winter in Rossendale can be a grim time, and when it began to set in that year Jim was convinced that my sheep would never survive the harsh climate. He suggested that it would be better to invest in a hardier breed instead. I hated to sell my sheep, but there was sound sense in what Jim was saying, so I went to Haslingden Auction Mart and invested the money from the Dorsets in forty Derbyshire Gritstone shearling ewes.

But for some reason I never did get on with those sheep and, after seeing some Herdwicks, Jim bought me a birthday present of six ewes and a ram from Charlie Relph, a farmer and sheepdog handler from Keswick in the Lake District. I was very taken with this breed for a time, but the ram was a terror for breaking out and the ewes were nearly as bad. We put up some very stout stock fencing, but my new sheep simply jumped over it like gazelles. After the ram had got as far as Burnley once — a distance of almost six miles — and tupped somebody's pedigree Suffolks on the way he became very fussy about the sheep he would mate with, viewing my ewes with a jaundiced eye and spending all his energies in finding escape routes. I think he had just grown used to females with a bit more class about them during his wanderings.

So, as I was not too popular for a time because of his misdemeanours, I eventually sold all the Herdwicks. After that I bought about fifty Swaledale ewes and borrowed a pedigree ram from Pop Hird, the

Swaledale ewe

well-known Swaledale breeder, who taught me a lot about this breed. I have always had Swaledales since that time.

It was during one lambing time at Jim's that I had an unforgettable and very unpleasant experience. All his land then was rented from the Water Board — it was poor pasture and very rough, so we could keep only a few sheep per acre, and it meant a lot of walking to get round it all. On this land there was a very deep pool, known locally as the Blue Lagoon, which I always checked every morning in case a ewe or lamb had fallen in.

One early morning, as I drew near to the edge of the pool, there was a heavy, dank mist swirling about which distorted everything around me. As it was barely light, it took me a few seconds to make out that there was something lying in the water. At first I thought it must be a ewe; then I decided that somebody was playing a joke on me, because floating on the surface was what looked like a tailor's dummy. I threw a couple of stones at it, and big bubbles rose to the surface. Then, as I drew closer, I realized to my horror that I was looking down at the corpse of a man, dressed only in a white tee-shirt with a length of material around the lower body. It was some seconds before I could move my legs, which felt as though they had decided to disown me. But eventually I managed to run down to the road, intending to flag down a car and get somebody to call the police. However, nobody would stop. Looking back, this is hardly surprising – I must have seemed a strange apparition, looming out of the mist in my balaclava, black overcoat and clogs and leaping up and down like a demented gnat. In the end, after what seemed like hours but was probably only a few minutes, a woman did stop and she raised the alarm.

As a skeleton had been found in the same place only a couple of years previously, I am sure that Jim and I were prime suspects for a short time. Indeed, the police asked us so many questions that we began to feel guilty, even though the finding of the body had been as much of a surprise to us as it had been to them. It eventually turned out that the dead man was a local lad who had punched his girlfriend. Her father had gone round to have a word with him, hit the lad on the head with a heavy pan and killed him. He had then disposed of the body in the pool. When it was pulled out of the water there were heavy chains round the legs – they had been attached to weights to keep the corpse at the bottom of the pool, but had later become detached, allowing the body to rise to the surface.

For weeks afterwards my imagination ran riot, especially in misty, foggy weather and after dark, and I could never bring myself to look into that pool again, even for the sake of the sheep and lambs. However, we did manage to raise a smile when, after one of the news photographers took pictures of us both looking down into the pool, a local wag was heard to comment, 'Those two would do anything to get into the papers.'

By the time I went up to Rossendale, Lad had returned home after his operation and was beginning to hobble around on three legs in the stable where he had his bed. He was uncomplaining and as friendly as ever, giving me an affectionate greeting before I kennelled Bonky Bill and Sykes for the night. When I went back into the house, Jim agreed that I should take over the job of helping Lad to improve his stamina and build up his muscles again to enable him to move around more freely. From that day onwards Lad has never been away from my side, and Jim eventually gave him to me when it became clear that the dog was going to overcome his disability and would be able to lead a useful life.

The first thing Jim taught me was that I must be much firmer with my dogs. Bonky and Sykes used to jump up at me in greeting (even Lad began to do this when he found he could get away with it), and I was ticked off as soon as Jim saw what was happening. 'You don't have to be cruel to your dogs. Just be firm and let them know that you mean what you say.' I was surprised that it was so easy to teach them good manners simply by pushing them down each time and refusing to make a fuss of them until they sat quietly in front of me. That simple lesson was the beginning of me becoming the leader of the pack. It was also the start of my success as a trainer.

I struggled on for some time with Sykes and Bonky; but, even with Jim's knowledge and guidance to help me, I knew the time was coming when I would have to make the decision to sell them if I ever wanted to get anywhere in the sheepdog world. In the end, my mind was made up for me when Sykes worried a sheep belonging to the farmer next door. Up to that time I had never tied up either of my dogs or put them in a kennel with a run to prevent them from wandering off, and I was confident that they would stay around the farmyard when they were not working. I should have known better because, whenever I had been out and drove back up the hill to the farmhouse, I saw this black dog wandering about on the hill. But Sykes knew the sound of my car, and by the time I drove into the yard he had run down to the bottom of the hill and jumped over the wall. I would find him lying near the house, eyes firmly closed as though he had been there for hours. Jim used to warn me that I ought to tie the dogs up or they would eventually be off worrying sheep – and, of course, that is exactly what happened. The incident made me realize that my dogs should be adequately kennelled at all times when they were not with me. It is irresponsible to let them wander about freely, and since then I have made every effort to provide a secure environment for all my own dogs and for those which come to me for training. The sad thing is that it took the violent death of a sheep to convince me that Jim had been right all along.

Both of my sheepdogs were sold shortly afterwards as farm dogs. Once they had gone off with their new owners, I was surprised to find that my main feeling was one of relief, tinged with the exciting prospect of looking for more promising material.

While I was steeling myself for the inevitable with my two dogs, Lad was making rapid progress. I started to take him for very short walks on flat ground, gradually increasing the distance as his legs grew stronger and he adapted to balancing on his remaining back leg. Then we began to go longer distances, taking in hilly ground and rough tussocks until the day came when, weeks later and with my heart in my mouth, I sent Lad off to gather some sheep standing a short distance away. I could hardly believe my eyes as I watched him run out to fetch his sheep in the way he had done when he ran out at the Subaru trial with Jim — the lack of a leg had done nothing to detract from his performance, and the only sign of his injury was that his back came up just a bit higher than before when he was running. When he walked up quietly behind the sheep, even I found it difficult to believe that this dog had only three legs, and my heart lifted. Lad's rehabilitation period had provided the pair of us with the chance to get to know each other really well — I now had a first-class dog with which to work, there was a strong bond between us, and the time had come for me to get on with my training as a handler.

One fundamental obstacle to improving my handling was the fact that I had still not learnt how to use the flat shepherd's whistle, and nobody seemed to be able to explain how to do it, either. If you have never seen one of these whistles, it consists of a flat, semi-circular sort of sandwich, about an inch and a half in diameter, with a small hole through the centre of the two layers and another hole at the back through which to thread a lanyard or string — this is then made into a loop which fits round the user's neck. Once mastered, this type of whistle is very easy to use and emits such a piercing sound that it can be heard over long distances in even the worst of weathers. The problem is learning how to get sounds out of it at all, and I had decided a long time back that the inventor of the shepherd's whistle must have had a warped sense of humour.

Jim's solution was to send me up on the fells with Lad. 'And don't bother coming home until you can whistle properly,' he called after me as I set off with my dog at my side, a shepherd's whistle hanging round my neck and a sandwich in my pocket. Jim had issued a challenge, and

I knew I had to rise to the occasion otherwise I would never hear the last of it. I could hear all the sheepdog men crowing because a woman was unable to do something which they found simple, and the thought of that was more than I could bear. 'I'll show him,' I muttered as I took myself out of sight. 'Even if I have to stay out all night to do it.'

What a performance it was! I blew, sucked, spat, swore, wept tears of despair and thought of walking off into the distance never to be seen again. I discarded the idea of drowning myself in the nearest tarn, asked Lad's advice, decided I would have to give up sheepdog handling because I would never conquer that stupid whistle, and then, just as I was becoming convinced that I was destined for the scrap heap, I produced a piercing whistle of the utmost clarity – the most beautiful sound I have ever heard. With no trouble at all I repeated the performance, and soon afterwards I could produce a variety of different sounds which would give me all the commands I needed.

Five hours after leaving Jim, I returned home in a state of euphoria and demonstrated my new-found prowess by getting Lad to go round the sheep, first to the left and then to the right. I thought I was making the same whistle commands for these movements that Jim had used with Lad, so I was surprised when I turned round to find Jim laughing at me.

'You've done really well. But do you realize that you've changed the tones of Lad's whistles completely?' he asked. 'What's amazing is that Lad's already relearnt them – he's adapted to the change without you knowing it.' And he was right – an example of how the intelligence and ability of these dogs can surpass that of the handler (and also an example of how we can inadvertently make mistakes which might confuse the dog).

Having worked only with Sykes and Bonky before going to Jim's, my developing partnership with Lad was a revelation to me. For the first time I had a dog with great natural intelligence and ability who was in a class of his own – he was well trained and delighted to be working again, and rarely put a foot wrong. Lad had an ability to work with any kind of sheep and knew instinctively how to handle them and how much pressure to put on them. It was an exciting time.

Every waking hour was spent working with the sheep, watching and learning from Jim, training my dog and going to sheepdog trials – by this time I was beginning to run Lad at some small local trials to get my hand in. Then, finally, Jim said it was about time I had a go at one of the big trials held in the area. I was still very nervous when I walked my dog out to the post, but I was at the point where I had to grit my teeth and get on with it if I was going to get anywhere at all.

A short time after this we went to the Holme sheepdog trials where Lad, now five years old, had quite a good run in the open class, although we were not placed – despite the fact that Jim was giving Lad one or two crafty commands from behind me when things were going wrong. Then (without any help from Jim this time) Lad and I won the Garstang Open Championship – a testing trial which is run over a big course on a steep hillside – and I knew we were getting somewhere at last. I learned afterwards that the judge had failed to notice that Lad had only three legs, which only goes to show how quickly and well the dog had adapted to his disability.

Throughout this time Jim and I were very happy, revelling in our time together, and everything seemed to be going our way. We were immersed in our shared interest with the dogs, spending a lot of time at trials and even more time out on the fells training our own and other people's dogs. There was rarely a time without a litter of puppies around the place, we had a lively social life in the farming community, and we shared a similar sense of fun and the ridiculous. So, in 1985, we decided to get married.

This time, the wedding was anything but conventional. Jim had no suit, so he borrowed one from his old mate Lawrence Yates. I hardly recognized him when he was all dressed up – he didn't look like the Jim I knew at all. He probably found me looking like a complete stranger, too, standing there in my long white dress; part of my outfit, however, was in its normal state – I had no suitable shoes to go with the dress, so I wore my wellies. Nobody spotted them until I got into the car! As there was a sheepdog trial that day, which we had no intention of missing, we had booked an early wedding at the Haslingden registry office, taking four friends as witnesses. Then we rushed back home to change into our jeans, boots and sweaters. After a quick celebratory drink and a sandwich at the local pub we were off, as competitive as ever and knowing that, for us, this was the best way of all to spend our wedding day! Of course, we had to put up with a lot of ribaldry from the other handlers who all knew what we had been up to. With their farmyard brand of humour they made comments which, although probably apt, are quite unprintable. It was a day full of laughter and one to remember.

5
I COME A CROPPER

When I married Jim I was twenty-four and had finally qualified to run a dog in the English National Sheepdog Trials. By this time Lad and I had developed a good partnership, being placed in trials on a regular basis. When I discovered that we had enough points to compete in a national-level championship (in the previous year, Jim and Lad had qualified to run in the English National but just failed to get into the English team for the International), I sent off to the International Sheepdog Society for the necessary forms. I filled them in and posted them off, thrilled to think that my clever dog would be running at the highest level. I felt confident that we stood a chance of winning (as I am sure did all the other 149 entrants) and looked forward to receiving our running order in due course.

Eventually, the brown envelope with the International Sheepdog Society's name on it dropped through the letter-box. It took some seconds for the reality of the enclosed letter to register before disappointment and anger took over. The neatly typed, impersonal sentences signalled the end of all my hopes of competing with Lad in my country's most prestigious championship. What it boiled down to was that Lad was not considered a suitable entrant because he had only three legs; when he came up to me and licked my hand, sensing my despair, I buried my face in his neck and wept.

Later, still seething with anger and bitterness, I took Lad out to the fell; as I watched him gathering the sheep more quietly and efficiently than many a sheepdog with four legs, my heart ached for him. I had looked forward to running him in the National, of course, but my main disappointment was on his behalf. I had wanted the sheepdog world to admire his prowess and bravery, his intelligence and achievement in the face of a terrible handicap triumphantly overcome — and a piece of official paper had wrecked those hopes forever. Being inordinately fond of my dog, I was so emotionally involved that it was to be some time before I was able to acknowledge that the Society might have been right in their decision — after all, dogs running at national and international level should be perfect physical specimens in order to enable the Society to promote this working breed. Lad's eyes had passed the required rigorous eye testing which meant that he was free of hereditary eye disorders, he had no genetic defects and he was a superb worker; but with only three legs he could not be called a perfect physical specimen, so that was that. However, the fact that the decision was correct did not alter my feelings at the time, and it still rankles — it is just that the passage of the years has enabled me to become more rational and charitable in my thinking.

Jim was very level-headed about it all, and when I had started to calm down he mentioned something which I had not even thought about when sending in the entry form. 'Lad's quite capable of running over the National course and of getting placed in the top fifteen. But that would mean he'd then be in the English team. So you'd take him to run in the International the following month, where the outrun is nearly twice as long. And he'd have to do two outruns, not one, to get all his sheep. That's a tall order for a fit, four-legged dog. But it's a near impossibility for Lad — he'd be so exhausted it wouldn't really be fair on him, if you think about it.' And, of course, Jim was right.

Jim's next move to stop me brooding was to encourage me to start looking round for a young dog to train. 'You're at a point where you ought to be training your own youngsters,' he announced. And so I began the search for a suitable young dog. I had become very confident in my handling of Lad, the dog who has taught me more than any other dog (or human being), but he was already trained when I acquired him and I knew that Jim was right. I needed to train a youngster from scratch, to enable me to put all my new-found knowledge into practice, if my skills were to develop further.

After marrying, Jim and I had moved to Windy Bank Farm, which stood in an exposed position on high ground about three miles from the small town of Rawtenstall (still in Rossendale). Our busy life continued as before, with both of us immersed in sheep and dogs and becoming increasingly competitive at trials. Jim is well liked by all the sheepdog people and there was a continuous stream of handlers coming to the house — buying dogs, selling them, showing off their prowess, discussing problems, successes and breeding lines. At first I used to keep quiet, because I still had so much to learn and felt that I was in no position to talk really knowledgeably about sheepdogs at that time. But I learned a lot by listening and watching.

One regular visitor was Richard Fawcett, the Yorkshire sheep farmer for whom I now work. He bought several dogs from Jim while I was at Windy Bank, and we also came across him at many of the trials we went to during that time. We began to visit Richard and his family regularly at their lovely farm in Hardraw, which is set in the middle of some of the most spectacular scenery in Yorkshire. After leaving Windy Bank, we would drive through the old Lancashire cotton towns of Burnley and Nelson before reaching the wild and beautiful open country of the Pennines. Then we continued north through the Dales, always enjoying the 40-mile journey whatever the season or weather. Over a period of time I got to know Richard and his wife, Anne, very well.

I had not been with Jim long before I met Mike Csernovits, the man who trained Lad before Jim had him, and who subsequently trained Cap — the dog which Jim later bought and with which he won the English National Championship in 1986. I think that Mike was probably the best trainer of young dogs I have ever met. He was also an interesting man with a long history of dog training — not only sheepdogs, but also guide dogs for the blind, tracker and guard dogs.

A naturalized Englishman, Mike was born in Budapest in 1935 of a Hungarian father, a successful racehorse trainer with his own stables near Budapest, and an English mother whose father, Bob Adams, was also a well-known horse trainer on the continent. In 1945 Michael's father sent his family to England because he disliked the Communist regime which was being imposed on his country. After schooling in England Mike did National Service with the Royal Army Veterinary Corps, training as a dog handler and serving in Malaya with guard and tracker dog units. He then joined Guide Dogs for the Blind, qualifying as a Grade 1 instructor, before going into farming.

Tot Longton's Jess

He fell in love with sheepdogs after a visit to Donnie Ross, a superb handler and trainer of Border Collies who works as a shepherd on a large estate at Kingussie in the Scottish Cairngorms. Mike always felt that training Border Collies for work and sheepdog trials was the supreme form of dog training, entailing co-operation from the dog not only close to hand, but also at a considerable distance from the handler and even, at times, out of sight. He bought his first Border Collies from the well-known handlers Tim Longton and John Holmes, and from then until his death was never without sheepdogs to train.

Eventually he rejoined Guide Dogs, working in the West Country, and his career with that organization developed alongside his increasing success with sheepdogs. His dog Mick was sired by Jim's famous dog Fleet, and bought by Mike at a few weeks old. Mike and Mick won the Devon and Exmoor Cup two years running, were placed second in the big Bath and West Show trials and also did well in smaller, local trials before Mike was promoted and left the area.

In 1983 Guide Dogs appointed him Regional Controller, North East, and this was followed by another move, in 1990, to the Oxford area to become Director of Operations for the United Kingdom. This last move pulled at Mike's heartstrings because he loved the North of England and its people; he had become well established there and had made many friends amongst those he considered to be the best sheepdog handlers in the world. Soon afterwards he became seriously ill, but he continued to train his dogs right up to the end and never lost his enthusiasm and zest for living — a brave and unforgettable man who taught me a lot about handling and training young dogs, and was always prepared to pass on his wealth of knowledge to others.

There is no doubt in my mind that Mike's greatest love was training young Border Collies for work with sheep, and one of the reasons he was so successful was undeniably his understanding of dogs and their behaviour. He had an uncanny knack of getting the best out of any youngster, and over the years he became respected throughout the country for the quality of the dogs he trained. Mike was a firm believer in giving his young dogs immediate, tasty rewards during training sessions. These were usually small, hard pieces of liver which his wife had cooked until it was crisp and dry, and Mike was never without a supply in his pocket. He said they helped the youngsters to concentrate their minds wonderfully. Having seen the results, I know that he was right.

After Mike's death I wanted to ensure that he would be remembered for his great contribution to the sheepdog world, so in January 1992 I set up the Mike Csernovits Memorial Open Trial at Hawes in Wensleydale. This will be an annual event, with a Challenge Cup presented by his widow. I only wish Mike could have been with us in 1992, but we all felt that he was there in spirit at least — particularly when a dog which he had trained was placed fourth with his owner, Gordon Hunt.

Another welcome visitor to Windy Bank was Ernie Brewer, from Rippendon near Halifax in Yorkshire. He had been a gundog trainer for years before he bought his first Border Collie bitch, Mist, from Jim, who taught him to train and handle her. Eventually, Ernie went on to breed and train sheepdogs with considerable success; he was always consistent and kind with his dogs, taking pride in their appearance and grooming them regularly. You always knew that a dog reared by Ernie would be a well-fed, happy animal which had been well socialized, and they were always in demand. Sadly, while competing at a nursery trial in March 1989 Ernie collapsed and died just as his dog was penning the sheep. The sheepdog world had lost yet another respected breeder and handler.

One day, Ernie arrived at our place with Royale Moss, a ten-month-old pup bred by John Winstone of South Wales, and I knew that I had found the dog I wanted. But Moss was not for sale and Ernie was impervious to persuasion, wheedling, bribery or feminine wiles. I had to swallow my disappointment and start looking elsewhere, but no dog compared favourably with Moss – he was a big, handsome, upstanding black and white collie with pricked ears and a big ruff round his neck. Search as I might, none of the other dogs I looked at seemed right. I was beginning to despair when Jim and I went off to a trial a few weeks later and saw Ernie there, once again with Royale Moss, and I went into the attack. Ernie must have had a moment of weakness, because he suddenly gave in to my badgering and agreed to sell Moss for £400. 'Done,' I said, and clinched the deal before he could change his mind. I took the dog home in triumph, despite the fact that I had never paid so much for an untrained dog before and could not really afford him. But I liked Moss so much that I would have gone without food for a month to get him (forgetting that Jim would have had to go hungry too!). The following morning Moss and I began to get to know each other, and before long I was able to begin his training in earnest. However, I was soon to realize that he would test my training abilities to the full in the months ahead.

Moss was intelligent, wayward, pushy and very strong when working the sheep. He preferred to work on his feet all the time, which was one of the things I liked about the dog, but he was difficult to stop and tended to move in too tightly when flanking – moving from one side of the sheep to the other. At such times I was able to put into practice some sound advice given to me by Glyn Jones. He explained how he goes about widening a dog's flanking movements and getting them really square, and I could hear his voice inside my head as I set to work with Moss. And what good advice it had been, because eventually Moss would flank off the sheep at right-angles every time and became a delight to watch.

By the end of the autumn I felt that Moss was ready to start his career, and I began entering him in the nursery trials which always take place during the winter months. But at the first trials we went to I discovered I was making a fundamental mistake. I was allowing Moss to watch some of the other dogs' runs before our turn was due, and he would get so excited and keyed up that he would then run badly. So at subsequent trials I kept him in the car, let him out to relieve himself well away from the trialling area, and then walked him quietly out to the post, talking to him calmly and reassuring him until I sent him off on his outrun. It worked, and after that we began to have some modest success.

I had also been making the mistake of entering my young dog in two or three nursery trials each weekend during the season. Nurseries are there to prepare a youngster for running in the open class when he is mature and able, and I was putting too much stress on him. I now ration the number of nursery trials in which I run my young dogs, and have found that they benefit in the long term. I had been expecting too much too soon.

I had to work very carefully with Moss and be firm with him all the time, first at nursery trials and later in the open class – especially when the sheep were wild Swaledales. He would be fine during the early part of his run, but by the time he reached the pen he would be so wound up that he would push the sheep right up to me, leaving us with no room to manoeuvre and causing the sheep to break away. All Moss's training during this time had to be exaggerated to teach him to flank squarely off his sheep, and it was something I had to keep reinforcing throughout the time he was with me.

While training and handling Moss I had to be even harder on myself than on my dog, because I soon discovered that raising my voice, becoming excited or, even worse, angry was completely counter-productive. Being a lively, enthusiastic, jumping-bean type of personality, it has meant a major adjustment for me to learn something which now seems second nature when handling dogs, but at that earlier time required a lot of conscious effort on my part.

At this time, 1985–6, Jim too was running his dogs successfully. He had two dogs which were both named Cap – one of which, Cap (142018), was destined to win the English National Championship with him in 1986 – and he also had a younger dog called Scot who was doing well at trials. I had Lad and Moss, and, with the other sheepdogs around the place, the sheep to look after and a busy trialling schedule, there seemed to be more than enough for the pair of us. Then Jim arrived home one day with a present for me – as it has turned out, one of the best I have ever had. Trim was to take me on to win many trials, including the *One Man and His Dog* Championship, screened in 1990. She and Lad are still my constant companions.

The first time I saw her, Trim was a four-month-old puppy on the end of a grotty piece of string held by Jim. A small bitch and the runt of a litter which had been bred by Jim Whaley of Widdale Side, near Hawes, she was further dwarfed by Jim's massive frame as she tried to hide behind his wellies. Jim had bought the pup from a dog dealer and given him £40 – a deal which included a sturdy kennel – so he was pleased with the transaction because she was from impeccable lines. As he handed the string over to me, Jim grinned and said if she failed to turn out well it would be due to my faulty training techniques. Another challenge!

From that moment on I thought the world of Trim, and from the first time I took her out to sheep, about a week later, I knew that she had something special about her. Nowadays I tend to leave a dog's work training until it is about a year old and raring to go, but with Trim I started harnessing her abilities right from the start because she was not only keen to go, but sensible and easy to handle. Jim knew straightaway that Trim had that something extra which makes a first-class dog. He said, 'You've got a blooming good bitch there, and you'll win more with her than with any dog you've had!' And Jim, who is a genius at picking out good dogs, was right.

Although Trim learned quickly and never challenged me in the way that Moss did, it was not all sweetness and light with her – there were times when she would run a bit wide, losing contact with her sheep. But I had enough experience by that time to know that we could get round this problem in time. She also had very little 'eye', and so could not dominate her sheep. But that problem, too, has disappeared as her confidence and maturity have developed, and she can now move any kind of sheep, no matter how much they try to defy her. She has become my right hand in any shepherding situation, and was destined to be one of the major attractions in the demonstrations which I began to give a couple of years later.

Because she made such rapid progress in her training, I was able to begin running Trim in the nursery trials of the winter of 1986–7 when she was only ten months old. She won or was placed in many of them, and generally made a name for herself. Some pessimists in the sheepdog fraternity began to shake their heads, predicting that her achievements would tail off when she started to run in the open class trials the following summer – this sometimes happens with dogs which are started off too young. But she continued to live up to her early promise, and did so well that she soon qualified to run in the English National Trials in 1988.

By now I had the training bit between my teeth. Shortly after Trim arrived John Stammers, a Wiltshire shepherd and great friend of Mike Csernovits, gave me Max, a puppy out of a litter sister to Lad, because he was so sad about Lad losing his leg. Once again I had acquired a dog which was completely different from any other I had handled, so when I began his serious training I had to feel my way with him and adapt my methods yet again to suit his personality. However, for various reasons Max was to be over a year old before I finally managed to get down to giving him the attention he needed.

In 1986, Jim and I had received an invitation to travel to Canada and the USA to judge trials, run training clinics and demonstrate our handling. Since this was my first visit to the New World, my excitement was intense as we boarded the plane for Toronto that September. We were met by Amanda Milliken, a successful sheepdog handler and triallist who had arranged for us to be on a coast-to-coast radio show. Jim and I enjoyed doing the interview, because the presenter asked us all the right questions and encouraged us to talk a lot about our dogs and sheepdog handling.

During the next few days, after judging a trial and running a training clinic, we set off with sheepdog handlers Jim and Ruth Clark on the three-hour journey to inspect another trial venue. On the way we visited the Niagara Falls, an unforgettable sight and every bit as awe-inspiring and beautiful as I had expected. The noise was unbelievable when we sailed right up to the waterfall itself in the boat appropriately named *Maid of the Mist*. Everybody else was wearing oilskins, but Jim and I preferred the feeling of being soaked by the curtain of spray which filled the air – an experience I will always remember. Afterwards, soaking wet and in the company of a crowd of Japanese tourists who all had cameras slung round their necks, we had a meal in the revolving tower which overlooks the falls and gives a fantastic view of the river and the surrounding countryside. To get there we all got into a glass-walled lift which started off at the bottom with no views but soon emerged into the daylight, revealing the most stunning scenery and causing us all to gasp at the sheer beauty of the place. The oohs! and ahs! sounded exactly the same in English and Japanese.

The morning after arriving at the Clarks' farm, Ruth cooked a huge breakfast of bacon and eggs for the four of us. She had it all laid out on a large platter and handed it to Jim with the intention of him serving himself before passing it round the table for everybody else to take their share. But Jim had other ideas and proceeded to tuck into the whole lot. I learned afterwards that Ruth was thinking, 'Gosh, he sure is a big eater,' while Jim was thinking, 'These Canadians do have large meals. I'll have to eat it all or Ruth will be offended.'

Jim Clark is the fifth generation to work his 150-acre farm. He and his father, Harry, grow seed corn, winter wheat and soya beans, keeping around twenty sheep on which to train their dogs and to use in their herding demonstrations. The small flock contains some Scottish Blackface sheep and some pure-bred Dorsets, which they find good for training the dogs and to provide freezer lamb and sheepskins. Jim took us on a tour of the area to see the variety of crops which are grown in Kent County, including seed corn, wheat, soya, tobacco, broccoli, peppers, tomatoes, apples, plums, cherries, peaches and grapes. I went up in Harry's little two-seater plane to get a bird's-eye view of the farm and the surrounding countryside. My stomach still lurches whenever I think about that hair-raising but exhilarating trip. Flying in a jumbo jet is very sedate by comparison.

On the Friday we were once again on the road, travelling this time to a place called Pleasure Valley for the next judging stint, then back to Clarksholme Farm for a late and rather rowdy supper with several of the competitors who had turned up in their campers and motorhomes. At six the following morning everybody, including such well-known handlers as Walt Jagger, Bruce Fogt, Bill Berhow, Mike Cannaday and Ralph Pulfer, set off to drive over the US border to Ohio for the next trial.

In no time at all, it seemed, our visit was over, although we managed to fit in one further engagement before boarding our plane in Toronto. Jim Clark was booked to do a demonstration in the city that same day, so we went with him so that I could do the commentary for him before a last-minute dash to the terminal. Although we had greatly enjoyed our visit and the new friends we had made, our journey home was sheer pleasure because every mile was taking us back to our dogs and competing in sheepdog trials again.

Barn door

By this time, late 1986, Jim and I had been together for nearly three years. Despite an auspicious beginning and some very happy times, things were gradually beginning to go wrong between us. At first I ignored the warning signs, throwing myself into training my dogs and travelling to trials with Jim. Once there we would be fine together, and I would think that I was imagining things – but I was only deluding myself. During and after the trials we would be in the beer tent, often ending the day by going with a group of handlers to a favourite pub for a meal and more booze. Gradually, without realizing it, we were both getting caught up in a vicious circle of drinking, very late nights, not enough sleep and too much work. I was no housewife and resented Jim's growing expectation that I should become one. Inevitably this led to frayed tempers on both sides, increasing irritation with one another's faults and, latterly, to some horrendous quarrels which nearly wrecked the pair of us.

It was during these months that we went over to some sheepdog trials in the Isle of Man. We had been invited to judge at one of the events and were intending to compete in the other. Everything went well to start with – the weather was good, and we enjoyed our day until we went to a nightclub with some of the other handlers. When a man came over and asked me to dance I was pleased because I love dancing, and thought nothing of it when I stood up to go to the dance floor. But Jim was not in the best of moods by this time, and he suddenly stormed out of the place. Unbeknown to me, he went straight off, caught the night ferry back to the mainland and went home to Rossendale, leaving me stranded on the Isle of Man with six dogs – three of mine and three of his.

I went to bed in blissful ignorance, assuming that Jim would be using another room in the hotel and would have calmed down by morning. At breakfast, of course, there was no sign of him, but I was still reasonably optimistic that he would be waiting on the quayside at 8 a.m. when I arrived to catch the ferry. With a sinking heart, I finally adjusted to the fact that I would somehow have to get myself, all the dogs and the luggage back home. I boarded the ferry in a less than affable frame of mind, and was even more angry by the time I landed on the other side – coping alone with six energetic working dogs on a two-hour sea crossing is no joke.

To make matters worse, I was unable to get hold of Jim when I phoned home. Eventually I managed to contact his sister, Yvonne, who has a great sense of humour. After laughing at my predicament she organized her son, Gordon, to collect me and take me home. By the time Gordon arrived I had been on the quayside, with dogs and luggage, for nearly six hours, so I was just about at the end of my tether when I arrived home to find that Jim was down at the pub with his cronies. The row which took place when Jim and I finally met up with each other was spectacular. Afterwards, the story did the rounds and everybody thought it was hilarious — so did I when I had calmed down, but I was furious at the time. We patched things up afterwards but, looking back, I now recognize that it was the beginning of the end for us.

Jim and I were still very fond of one another (and, now that it is all over, we still are), but were finding it increasingly difficult to live together without inflicting the most vindictive hurt of one kind or another. I was very upset, as I am sure Jim was, and when out with friends tried to behave as though there was nothing wrong. I was unable to get Jim to discuss our problems, and was beginning to feel cut off from him and lonely. This led to my flirting outrageously with the men in our immediate social group (and denying I was doing so) which would hurt Jim even more. And so the vicious circle of drinking and immature behaviour continued until the day when I walked out and took myself off to stay with Viv and Geoff Billingham, the well-known sheepdog handling couple who were then living and working in Beaumont Water, near Yetholm in Scotland.

The Billinghams were very kind to me, although I must have been depressing company during the month that I stayed with them. Our shared interests in shepherding, breeding sheepdogs, training and trialling helped me to to get myself back on a more even keel once again. I had to return to Rossendale on business at the end of that time and was met at the station by Jim. We were so pleased to see each other again that we kissed and made up, laughing together as we had done in our early days and both certain that our love for each other would enable us to overcome any future difficulties. But it was not to be, and I left Jim for good the following year, angry, sad, frightened and once again unsure of myself. All my confidence in my abilities was completely shattered, and I was uncertain what the future might hold in store.

6
IN LIMBO

The only things I took with me at the end of my marriage to Jim were my dogs, Lad, Moss, Trim and Max, and my crooks. Once again, good friends in the sheepdog world took me in at a desperate time and were so helpful that I will never be able to repay them for their kindness. One of these was Jan Taylor, who had given me a lot of help and an understanding ear before I left Jim. She and her husband, Alan, had a farm near the old Roman village of Ribchester, about 14 miles from Windy Bank, and they put me up at their home for the night when I finally walked out. Jan is a very lively person, good at imitating dialects and accents, mad about sheepdogs, and we get on well together; Alan, however, is possibly a bit wary of me because he thinks I might be a bad influence and lead his wife astray. Jan has a loopy sheepdog called Taff and would like to handle dogs to help with the farm work, but she is always too soft with them. Inevitably they take advantage, with the result that she never gets very far with their training!

The following day I went south to the sheepdog handler Julie Deptford and her husband, Dick, who had invited me to stay with them on their farm in March, Cambridgeshire, while I got myself sorted out and looked for a job. I had first met Julie at a trial in Derbyshire and realized then that she was a superb handler, acknowledging that she would probably be better than me eventually because she has a strong personality and more natural authority. I did wonder, at the time, how I would react if another woman came along and did well in trials – with my competitive nature I have invariably striven to be the best. It was a relief to find that it does not worry me at all. Some time later, Julie and Dick bought a farm in Scotland and she began to compete in the trials up there, eventually winning the Scottish National Trials in 1991 and the Farmers' Championship when she captained the Scottish team at the International Trials later in the year. I was delighted for her, and pleased that she was the first woman ever to achieve those two trophies. But I must admit to a feeling of relief when she came second in the *One Man and His Dog* competition the same year – up to that time I had been the only woman to win it, and I was not yet ready to give up my coveted position! I am human, after all, but I wish her good luck in the future – she is certain to win it one day.

Julie and I have very different personalities, but we both possess the single-mindedness and determination needed to succeed. She is quieter and more introverted than I am, but is equally wrapped up in sheep, sheepdogs and trialling. Another thing we have in common is the fact that she is not from farming stock but married a farmer's son who had inherited his father's farm.

While I was staying with Julie, we went to some trials together in East Anglia – they were well organized, with a high standard of handling, although I doubt if the competition was quite as strong as in the north. I did not do at all well at those trials; my unhappiness and loss of confidence affected my handling, I was getting very nervous again when going out to the post to compete, and my dogs were reacting badly. Added to these problems was the fact that I was running out of money and still had no job. It was then that I sold Royale Moss – one of the biggest mistakes I have made in my career with dogs, and something I have regretted ever since. Glyn Jones told me later that he could not believe it when he heard what I had done because Moss was just coming into his prime and, before I left Jim, I was beginning to have considerable success with him at trials.

Moss was later shipped out to the USA after being bought by a handler called Lena Bailey. He eventually returned to compete in this country when Lena decided to live in Britain and settled in mid-Wales, bringing her team of dogs with her and entering the sheepdog trialling scene over here. So I still have contact with Moss by watching Lena run him at trials – and still wish I had never sold him. The dog which won *One Man and His Dog* in 1992 was T.C. Evans's Nap – a son of Royale Moss and Trim. It gave me a lot of pleasure to have bred that top-class dog from two of my favourite collies.

Blue-faced Leicester tup

The first job I had after leaving Jim was near Thetford in Norfolk, where another shepherd and I had the task of looking after five thousand store lambs – mainly Suffolk cross-breds being fattened for slaughter – and about sixty mule ewes – half-breds which in the north are usually from a Swaledale ewe and a blue-faced Leicester tup. The farm belonged to the Abery family and was run by two brothers: Chris, who was in charge of the arable side, and Robert, who was responsible for the livestock. It was a well-run farm, with some impressive portable equipment which could be taken to the flock whenever we needed to treat the sheep, and I enjoyed this part of the work. However, although I liked the people I was working for, I hated most of my time there because the sheep were run on a strip-grazing system. It nearly drove me crackers. With this type of shepherding, the animals are moved from one patch of grazing to another every few days, which entails erecting and taking down electric fencing each time the flocks are moved. It played havoc with my temper (and my hands!). That was when I found out that electric fencing, even when highly charged, does not necessarily keep the animals in check; many a time I would find that a cheeky lamb had discovered that it could get its neck under the wire and ease itself out. When this happened, it was invariably followed by most of the rest of the flock. A lot of hard work was then needed to get them all back within the fencing once again. The trouble is that, once sheep have learnt how to foil the system, they will do it time and again afterwards, exasperating the shepherd when he or she finds them grazing on land (often that of the neighbouring farm) which was not intended for that purpose.

The only dogs needed for this kind of work were rough and ready farm types to help in the pens when dosing the sheep or treating their feet — not good work at all for a well-trained sheepdog, which, if asked to do this type of thing all the time, with little gathering and other tasks to provide a balance, would develop bad habits. As a result, my dogs were getting bored. They were also out of condition without adequate hill work to keep them fit, despite the fact that Robert allowed me to keep a small flock of sheep on his land for training purposes. The flatness of the landscape was a problem for me, too. I soon began to miss the beauty and challenge of the mountains and fells with which I had always been surrounded. Everything in the Norfolk method of sheep farming seemed to be rushed and impersonal, and I was missing the steady rhythm of hill shepherding and the pleasurable task of training my dogs for the skilled work needed in mountainous country. In short, I was getting homesick.

While working in Norfolk I lived in a cottage belonging to Jane and Roger Thornton — a farming couple who were to become the sort of friends with whom I will always keep in touch. Roger is a man with a great personality, born into farming, and has an ability to work and play hard. His wife is also a very sociable person but from a totally different background — when they met she was a fashion model, and she still looks like one with her trim figure and long black hair. Jane's attractive appearance and elegant, well-manicured hands made me ashamed of my own hands, which were always chapped and ingrained with dirt after daily handling of the electric fencing. She and Roger used to tease me about it and as a Christmas present that year gave me a huge tin of Swarfega — the gooey green grease-removing jelly favoured by car mechanics.

Roger prefers arable to stock farming, so he could understand my dislike of strip grazing on flat grassland. He knew my preference was for hill shepherding, and he gave me a lot of encouragement to keep training my dogs and to get back to the mountains as soon as I could. I am convinced that his kindness was instrumental in helping the five of us retain our sanity during the six months we stuck with the job at Thorpe Farm.

The Thorntons' farm is all arable land, and they had no animals except for their dogs: two old but very lively Jack Russell terriers, Pippin and Plogsey; Tilt, a black Labrador trained to the gun; and a young English Springer spaniel named Wally, who lives up to his name and is a great character. Jane and Roger have a shoot on their farm two or three times a year in the game season, with everybody ending up in the local pub, the Larling Angel, by the end of the day — Roger belongs to a group of farmers who take it in turns to host shoots on their land, and this leads to a full social life with friends who have similar interests.

The farmhouse is a huge Georgian pile with tall windows, high ceilings and beautifully proportioned rooms. The dining room comes into its own when feeding the members of the shooting party. I enjoyed helping Jane on those days, and have a vivid memory of walking into the kitchen once to find Wally standing on the long wooden table with his feet straddling the piles of plates which had been put out ready to go into the dining room. While I stood there with my heart in my mouth and wondering how to get him off without wrecking Jane's expensive china, Wally, normally a clumsy, rather unco-ordinated dog, began to move his feet with the utmost delicacy, leaving a trail of muddy paw marks before jumping down to the floor and running to greet me.

Although I disliked the type of farming carried out in the flat countryside of Norfolk I loved the people there, and made many friends in a short space of time. Among them was Sheilah Ellis, who lives some distance away in a village in Leicestershire. I met her for the first time in the beer tent at the English National Sheepdog Trials and our friendship has grown steadily since then, despite the thirty-year difference in our ages and the fact that these days we are only able to get together occasionally.

The sheepdog handler Eric Elliott, and his wife, Jen, had told me a lot about Sheilah before I met her. Even so, I was unprepared for the impact which her quirky, sensitive personality and sense of humour were to have on me. Sheilah, who has spent her whole life working with sheep and cattle, is still employed as a shepherdess. She developed her love of animals as a small child and used to help her farming father with his stock. As soon as she was old enough she left school and during the Second World War joined the Women's Land Army, not telling them that she was under age. Her first job as a wartime 'Land Girl' was as a shepherdess, working for a farmer who was also a cattle and sheep dealer. Having worked in the Land Army for seven years, Sheilah was one of three hundred Land Girls who were invited to London to meet the Queen (now Queen Elizabeth the Queen Mother). After that she returned to the shepherding which has been her life's work.

For most of the year Sheilah now works alone with a flock of five hundred mule ewes, but she has the help of an agricultural student throughout lambing and says that she enjoys the company of young people at those times. Like most shepherds, Sheilah finds lambing time the most rewarding part of her working year. She enjoys her close contact with the sheep as she helps to deliver their lambs, revelling in the satisfaction of a job well done at the end of the season when she and her dogs can return to a more steady pace of life.

Sheilah has always had sheepdogs to help her in her work, and enjoys watching the handlers at local sheepdog trials whenever she can spare the time from her busy schedule – although she has never competed herself. In many ways – apart from the obvious one that we are both shepherdesses – Sheilah and I have much in common. She was featured in a television film with Phil Drabble when the cameras recorded her activities during lambing time – later shown during one of the *One Man and His Dog* series – and she has also been a guest at three Women of the Year luncheons at the Savoy Hotel. We share a similar sense of humour and are both partial to a tot when relaxing after a hard day's work. Sheilah is also in great demand as an after-dinner speaker. And, of course, we both love sheepdogs and sheep.

*

Having started the Norfolk job in June 1987, I stayed there until just before Christmas. Then I received the news that my father had had a heart attack, so when I went over to North Wales to visit him in hospital I gave in my notice.

My father's sudden illness was a shock to all the family because he had always been such a healthy, vigorous man. When the consultant announced that his only chance of living more than a short time was to have a triple by-pass, the world seemed to stand still for a while. Fortunately the operation was successful, but Dad had to retire early which was a pity after all the hard work he had put into the school over the years.

While Dad was ill I saw a different side to my mother, who was amazingly strong and supported him so well throughout his illness that he would never have dared to die! Now my parents live happily in a cottage in North Devon, where I visit them whenever I can get down there. My father has been able to adapt well to his new life and still acts as a consultant to the headmaster and governors of St David's, maintaining links with his old life without the stresses and strains inherent in a responsible full-time job – a godsend for him, because it gives him an interest and a focus for his talents.

Shortly after my arrival in Norfolk I started going out with Roger's son, Andy. He had no interest in farming and went off to Andorra in the Pyrenees in the late autumn to work in a bar and ski in his spare time. Dad's condition was steadily improving, so I decided to take Andy up on his suggestion that I should join him after Christmas. I went back to the cottage, spent Christmas with Jane and Roger, sold my litter of puppies out of Trim, and then set off for the holiday of a lifetime. I was only able to make such a decision because I had good friends who were encouraging me to take a long holiday and who were prepared to look after my dogs while I was away. Just before Christmas Richard Fawcett had offered me a lambing contract on his farm, to begin on 1 April. I had three months with no commitments, and I decided to make the most of them.

When I flew out to Andorra I intended to stay there for four weeks – but I ended up spending over two months there, having a whale of a time. Not that I was much good at ski-ing – Dad had taken me to Austria for a winter holiday several years earlier and, despite my love of sport and physical challenge, most of my time was spent flat on my back in the snow with my skis up in the air. I soon discovered that the passage of time had done nothing to improve my powers of concentration and co-ordination as I optimistically set off down the ski slope, only to land in an ungainly heap at the bottom each time. But I did keep trying, to much amused comment from onlookers, and I greatly enjoyed the social side.

By the end of the first month, my money was beginning to run out. At the same time the cook at the Asterix bar in Arinsal, where Andy was working, managed to break a leg and a replacement was needed at short notice. It is probably a measure of the desperation the owner was feeling that I was able to persuade him to appoint me to fill the gap. Most of the time I managed to do well, although there were one or two occasions which convinced me I am not really cut out for such an occupation.

The first disaster occurred when I had just drained a cauldron full of spaghetti. As I was lifting the pan from the stove to the table, just before serving up the spaghetti to a large coach party which was waiting to be fed, the pan tipped and its contents slid gracefully on to the tiled floor. I scooped it all back into the pan with such speed there was no time for dirt to adhere to the strands (or so I kidded myself) — and, most importantly, nobody else in the kitchen had noticed, so I carried on as though nothing had happened.

The other mistake I made turned out to be a blessing in disguise and affirmed my local fame as a cook. Each day, I made a fridge cake, which Andy would cut into slices to sell in the bar. This cake was well-laced with brandy and tasted delicious, so it always sold well. One day, without my noticing it, the top of the brandy bottle fell into the cake mixture. The first thing anybody knew about it was when a customer brought it up to the bar counter to complain. Fortunately I was on the ball, and did a bit of quick thinking — I congratulated the man on winning the day's free double cognac. He went away happy with his balloon glass half full of brandy, and for the rest of my time there a (clean) bottle top was mixed into the fridge cake each day: customers would clamour for their slice in the hope of finding the bottle top and winning a free drink. That venture probably reduced the hotel's bar profits but helped me to save face — and it certainly trebled the sales of my fridge cake.

By the end of two months in Andorra I was feeling much more relaxed and happy and was beginning to feel that, although I still missed Jim, I would be able to live a full life again without him. However, despite all the activity and lively social life at the ski resort, I was without regular contact with animals, especially dogs and sheep, and was eagerly looking forward to returning to England to start work on my lambing contract with Richard at the end of March. Then, three weeks before I was due to fly home, Richard phoned to tell me that he had injured his back and to ask if I could start work with him immediately. I was so excited at the prospect of returning to shepherding that I dropped everything, said goodbye to Andy and took the first available flight to England. As soon as I got back I collected my dogs, who gave me the welcome of a lifetime and so much affection it made me wonder how I had been able to leave them with other people for so long. Then, two days later, we all travelled up to Yorkshire, at the start of something which was to be a major turning point in my life.

7
DALES FOLK

As soon as I arrived in Wensleydale I became immersed in all the tasks which have to be done immediately before lambing. After gathering all the sheep from the fells and bringing them down to the home pastures, my dogs and I soon began to slim down and build up the stamina we would need to get through the next few busy weeks. The holiday had done us all good in our different ways — after their enforced rest, Lad and Trim were in fine fettle and eager to get back to sheep work. Because Max was still untrained I was unable to use him for work, so his holiday lasted until the end of lambing when I planned to begin his training.

My first lambing contract with Richard was a complete delight from start to finish and, as I became immersed in work, my holiday in Andorra faded rapidly into the past in the face of the harsh realities of a Dales lambing. It was the first time I had ever worked on a hill farm which had such a high standard of stockmanship: everything was clean, well organized and in good order. The ewes had been carefully fed in the weeks before lambing, which meant they were in the best condition possible to help them to cope with their offspring (and the weather if it turned bad), and I was learning so rapidly that the days seemed to fly past. This was the time when I began to develop real sheep sense — an essential commodity if I was to become a top-class sheepdog handler. Richard can (and does) tell many tales about my work in the sheep pens after I arrived: I was hopeless. People born into shepherding have a big advantage over those like me who come into the game late — we have a lot of catching up to do.

A Dales barn

In 1988 we had one of the wettest lambing seasons I can remember, and I have vivid memories of continually having to move soaking wet ewes and their shivering lambs into the shelter of the barns and the stone walls to minimize the effects of cold winds combined with incessant rain. Every shepherd dreads this situation, because it increases the incidence of pneumonia and prevents the new-born lambs from drying out sufficiently for their fleeces to become waterproof. But there were also a few days when the bad weather eased, making the task a little lighter and lifting everybody's spirits until the rain closed in again.

Like my mother, I have always been an early riser. Getting out of bed before dawn was therefore no problem, particularly when I was greeted with the reward of red- and yellow-streaked skies as the sun began to rise, and then watched the ribbons of mist swirling slowly over the valley bottom before they gradually evaporated in the rising temperature. Even the grey, wet early mornings had their rewards as

I set out with my dogs to check the ewes and lambs, quietly working amongst them and moving them to shelter where I would feed them before going on to the next field.

Lad had already proved himself as a good lambing dog at Jim's, but it was Trim's first season with ewes and lambs. With her quiet and gentle nature I knew she was unlikely to upset the flock, but I was not certain how she would react with sheep if they turned on her to protect their young. As it turned out, Trim was rather wary at first, and I had to encourage her to stand her ground if she was to turn a defiant ewe. But she soon began dealing with mothers and offspring as though she had been doing it all her life, and by the end of the six weeks had become as indispensable as Lad. Being able to use two dogs for the job meant that I could occasionally give one of them a day off to prevent them becoming tired and stale, and this did wonders for their stamina and concentration. I also found that they needed much more food during the four weeks when they were working extra-long hours; even so, they were considerably thinner at the end of lambing than they had been at the beginning.

Throughout this time I was living in the farmhouse at Hardraw with Richard and his family, and my friendship with Anne really began to blossom. I also found that I loved their four children, who are all very bright and lively. It was the first time I had ever lived at close quarters with youngsters, and it was a revelation to me to find I could enjoy their company so much. I think my time with training young animals must have taught me something about dealing with young human beings, because I soon realized that many of the same principles apply – quiet, firm handling, a consistent approach, the giving of affection, endless patience and a shared acknowledgement about who is the boss. Once we had this sorted out we got along famously.

Until I met Anne Fawcett I had only had a few close female friends. I then became friendly with her sister-in-law, John Fawcett's wife, who is also called Anne. This causes endless problems, and so that readers do not become equally confused I shall call John Fawcett's wife Anne (J) and Richard Fawcett's wife Anne (R)! Being such a tomboy as a child, and based in a boys' school, I had always wanted to be a boy and invariably gravitated towards male company. Once I even chopped off my long, thick plaits to make me look more like a boy – it was an unnerving experience which not only upset my parents but also frightened me to death because I looked such a mess. Up to my mid-twenties I was continually falling in and out of love, which left little time for female friends, so to find that I could enjoy other female company came as a pleasant surprise to me and I now greatly value my friendships with members of my own sex. No longer do I pine to be a male in a man's world (it is much more fun being a woman in a man's world) and I now enjoy the intelligence, humour and flexible approach to life demonstrated by my female companions. I have not given up men altogether, because I still like them too − it is just that there is now a better balance.

Shortly after lambing came to an end Richard, who already had one permanent shepherd on the farm, told me he did not have sufficient work to keep me on. So I began to look round for another job, and put an advertisement in the northern newspapers. Within a couple of days I had a telephone call from a man with a Teesdale accent from County Durham, some 20 miles north of Hardraw, who was looking for a good, hard-working shepherd. 'I live with me mother and five thousand sheep,' he said. Now five thousand sheep is a huge number for one shepherd (six hundred would be more realistic), but as I was so eager to get a job I told him that was fine, assuring him that I was a hard worker. He went on, 'We need somebody who can cook for us.' 'I'm a very good cook,' I lied. Even when the farmer told me I would have to go to church twice on Sundays I bravely told him it would be no problem. It was only when he ended up by asking, 'Canst 'ee lend us a pund?' that I realized my mysterious caller was Tommy Brownrigg, a well-known North Country handler with a penchant for pulling people's legs.

A short time after Tommy's phone call I found a job just a couple of miles from Hardraw. I started work there at the beginning of May, living in with the family and milking every morning, and doing shepherding work through the day. The farmer did the evening milking, which meant I had sufficient time to myself in the summer evenings to go over to Richard's to train my dogs. This all seemed an ideal arrangement to me, but it was not long before it began to dawn on me that the farmer's wife was not happy about my presence on the farm, probably because I was a young female working at close quarters to her husband. In fact she had no grounds whatever for jealousy — it was the job I loved, not her old man! Whatever the reason, the atmosphere eventually became so tense that I went to the farmer and offered to leave. He told me, 'I don't want you to go because you're such a good worker, and I have no complaints about that at all — but my family life has been hell since you arrived, and I don't think I can stand the strain any longer.' So the farmer and I parted friends, although I had unwittingly made an enemy of his wife.

Meanwhile, change was afoot at Richard's farm. Anne had been offered a mature student place on a year's foundation course at a college in Harrogate, to be followed by a three-year art degree course at Hull. This meant she would be away from home on weekdays during termtime for the next four years. When she and Richard suggested that I might move back to Hardraw and look after the children while Anne was at college, I jumped at the offer. 'You're really good at training dogs,' Richard told me. 'It's what you want to do, and I think you should start to train dogs for other people as a small business venture. As long as you're around the place when the children need you, then you can spend as long as you like with the dogs. And you can keep your own small flock on my land to provide you with quiet sheep for starting off the youngsters. And, of course, there's always a lambing contract for you each year.' After my experience at the other farm, it was a relief to find there were still pleasant, trusting people around. Once again the help and generosity of friends was to give me confidence and enable me to do my own thing.

Although I was not fully aware of it at the time, I now know that the opportunity given to me by Richard and Anne, and their continual encouragement to set up in my own business, was a major turning point in my life which has been largely responsible for the happiness and success I have enjoyed since then. They gave me stability and enabled me to put down roots for the first time since leaving my parents' home. During this time I have been able to move into my own cottage, and my increasing self-confidence has led me to enjoy living there without feeling that I have to have a man around to look after me. In other words, I have done a lot of growing up.

By the early autumn I had moved back in with the Fawcett family, and things began to happen which would eventually result in my becoming firmly established as a shepherdess, sheepdog trainer and demonstrator.

I placed an advertisement in the *Farmer's Guardian*, and during my first weekend back at the Fawcetts' farm I think Richard and Anne began to wonder if they had done the right thing — the phone never stopped ringing for the first two days, during which I had over seventy enquiries from people who wanted their dogs trained. Richard had always said he thought there would be a good response, but I doubt if even he had appreciated its full potential.

Since that time I have always had dogs in for training, and have packed more experience into the past four years than I might have acquired in twenty if I had just been training my own dogs. At first I would take up to ten dogs at a time, but soon found that this was too many when I also had my own dogs to train. Then, when the demonstrations started, I had to limit the numbers even more, especially during the show season. Now I usually have up to three or four dogs to train, in addition to my own. I find this keeps me busy while allowing me enough time to give the dogs the individual attention they need.

My experience was also growing in other ways. I found myself enjoying my work as nanny to the Fawcett children — they were bright youngsters, quick to accept me as part of their everyday lives. Anne was at home every weekend and during the college holidays to look after them, and the weekdays passed so quickly that they never resented the fact that she was not there full time. It is difficult to believe, at the time of writing, that Anne has only a few months to go before taking her degree and then it will all be over — the time has passed very quickly, and much has happened in those four years to change all our lives in one way or another.

Richard's father, Dick, lives across the road with his wife, Mamie, so they are able to see a lot of their grandchildren and keep an interest in the farm. They too have accepted me into the family group as though I had been born and bred in the Dales, so perhaps it is hardly surprising that Wensleydale has now become the place where I feel most at home.

Dick, who is now seventy-three, has a strong, likeable personality and it was only in 1991, after thirty years working there, that he retired from his job as manager of the Hawes Auction Mart. In addition, he has been a director of the Mart for forty-eight years and chairman for twenty-seven of those years — quite a record. It was after Richard returned from Newton Rigg Agricultural College to start taking on the farm work and management that Dick was able to concentrate on his work at the Mart, which was really the love of his life.

One of Dick's greatest friends is Jack, now Richard's right-hand man at the farm and previously Dick's, with never a cross word in all their forty-two years together. Dick and Jack are still the best of friends, and when Jack also retires at the end of 1992 it will seem like the end of an era. These two men have witnessed great changes in the Dales farming scene over the years, have contributed to the farming economy for more than half a century and, even in retirement, will still make a contribution when extra pairs of experienced hands are needed on the farm. Even in their seventies, they can still teach the youngsters a thing or two.

Dick has a prodigious appetite which is famed throughout Wensleydale, and has a great liking for beef, to which Mamie panders by cooking what seems like half a cow each week. With so much protein intake Dick is still amazingly strong, with great energy which would put many a younger man to shame.

Every year, Dick and I go together in his car over the fells to the annual Swaledale Sheep Breeders' Association meeting which is held at the church hall in Muker. It's an odd set-up. I'm the only woman among all these Dalesmen who have spent their lives with sheep — not that I recognize any of them on this particular day. I'm used to seeing them in their battered and muddy working clothes, but for this occasion they all dress up and they seem like different people altogether. It's not a very exciting get-together, and when I'm bored I can't help but show it. Dick gets very cross with me because when the tedium gets too much I just get out my pad and pencil and start sketching — the meeting may be dull, but the characters and their expressions are anything but. Perhaps it would be more interesting if people got up and argued — but the strange thing is that nobody ever says anything at these meetings. Afterwards, when we all assemble at the Farmers' Arms, things are very different: then everyone has his say, and in no uncertain terms!

Having said that, I suppose I should be grateful to have got to the meeting at all. The ride there is an event for which I need to prepare myself, because I am scared out of my wits by Dick's driving. My first experience of it came one lambing time, when he took me in his Land Rover to check some ewes. The sheep were grazing below Shunner Fell on the High Pasture, a field on a very steep hill. Nobody in their right senses ever drives down that hill – they always go round it – but Dick does not allow himself to be encumbered with ordinary mortal fears. As we reached the top of the hill, I was taken by surprise when Dick shouted, 'Shut your eyes, lass,' before pointing the vehicle downhill and putting his foot down. We went down that field at the speed of light, in fourth gear and with barely two wheels on the ground. The dogs in the back were thrown all over the place, hitting their heads on the roof as we nearly took flight, while I sat glued to the front seat in rigid fear.

As soon as the Land Rover stopped at the bottom of the hill, I leaped out and found myself trembling from head to foot, my knees buckling with terror as I took a huge swig from my hip flask. Much to Dick's amusement I refused to get back into his vehicle and, having checked the sheep, set off for the walk home. I had decided that, if Dick wanted to kill himself, he could do it without my company. My fears were not unfounded. Shortly before I moved to Wensleydale, Dick turned the Land Rover completely over in the remote High Pasture and was trapped in it, with his dog, Tweed, for several hours before he managed to struggle free and get Tweed out.

I suspect Dick must be particularly accident-prone. A few years ago there was another incident which might have proved fatal if he had been on his own at the time. He and Richard were dipping sheep in a 400-gallon dip tub when a ram lunged forward, knocking Dick off balance. He landed head down in the tub with the ram on top of him and his feet sticking out above the dip fluid, which is a very toxic mixture. As the tub is deep and narrow it was difficult for Richard to manoeuvre his father into an upright position, and it took several seconds in the confined space. When Dick had finished coughing and spluttering he was sent off to have an immediate bath while his son rang for medical help.

Dr King duly arrived, examined Dick and pronounced him alive and well. 'He'll be OK,' he said. 'It'll certainly clean out his nose for him.' And, being a man who never wastes time on unecessary details, he was off. Dick's main concern was not for his health but for his spectacles, which had fallen off into the dip tub and were sitting on the bottom where nobody could reach them, being attacked by the dip fluid. The tub had to be drained before rescue was effected and Dick was happy again.

Lleyn ewe and Lamb.

I always tease Dick about the way he handles Tweed. He is inconsistent and shouts all his commands in the same tone and so loudly that they can be heard for miles around, even though the dog may be working close to hand. Half the time the poor animal is not sure whether he is coming or going, but he remains faithful to Dick and would die for him — a long-suffering dog who wants to please.

Dick still lives for the Auction Mart and spends most of his time there, even though he is supposed to be in retirement. It was Dick who made it the successful, thriving selling centre it is today, and it is there that he regularly meets up with all his old cronies as they stand around the ring, casting knowledgeable eyes over the animals for sale and swopping jokes and gossip. Another place where they all congregate is in the canteen at the Mart — a spotlessly clean establishment run by Big Doreen, who cooks huge meals for her clientele and can give as good as she gets from the farmers and shepherds who now regard her as a local institution.

Dick's Tuesdays are always earmarked for going to the Auction Mart, and nothing is ever allowed to interfere with this, the most important day of his week. His Fridays are supposed to be set aside for a day out with Mamie, but Dick hates shopping and is always looking for an excuse to prevent him from going to Darlington or any other town which Mamie wants to visit. As a result he has become addicted to attending funerals — especially those which take place on a Friday. If he goes away for a weekend or a week's holiday in Scarborough with Mamie, the first question he always asks after returning to Wensleydale is, 'Has anybody died?'

Recently, a farmer from Derbyshire came to the Auction Mart to buy some suckler cows. The last time he had been in Hawes was seventeen years before. As he walked into the ring, he caught sight of Dick standing with his stick and was overheard to say, 'Ee, that old man's still here.' As Dick must have been in his early fifties (and certainly not old by farming standards) when the man last saw him, the remark caused a lot of laughter as the story spread.

The majority of my Dales friends are members of the farming community, but there are some exceptions. Amongst these is Big Dave, who used to have a courier business in London but tired of the rat race and bought a house in Hawes where he now lives with his partner, Nina, and their small daughter, Naomi. Big Dave is an apt name for this hefty, bearded bear of a man whose sense of fun, combined with a likeable personality, great integrity and intelligent, individual approach to life have ensured his acceptance amongst the locals. He is a photographer with an infinite knowledge of the technical side of the trade and he and Nina, who is a graphic designer, are planning to go into business together, combining their artistic skills in work they will both enjoy. The pride of Big Dave's life is his enormous Harley Davidson motor-bike and he is now a familiar sight as he roars around Wensleydale with his family, well wrapped up against the cold and ensconced in the roomy sidecar.

In the summer of 1991 there were so many untrue tales about me doing the rounds in the Dales that I decided to give wagging tongues something to keep them happy. Big Dave and Nina laughed when I told them my plan, and arrangements were made for the following weekend. Early on Saturday morning I climbed into Big Dave's sidecar with my dogs at my feet, crook wedged at my side and sticking out the back as we set off for the first trial of the day. Never having travelled in this way before

I found the journey rather hairy, but it was well worth it as we zoomed noisily on to the trials field, shattering the peace of the countryside. Of course, everybody thought the worst and their faces were a picture. Heaven knows what they would have thought if we had put the other part of the plan into practice. Nina was to be brought to the trials field later in a friend's car. She would then leap out and run over to me, hitting me about the head and accusing me of stealing her man. But the three of us had decided this would be taking things too far, and we had chickened out at the last minute.

Another well-known personality in Hawes is Tot Iveson, who has been a livestock dealer there since he left school. Now sixty-four, Tot bought his first four sheep when he was ten years old: they cost him 2s 6d (12½p) each. After keeping them on pasture for six weeks he sold them for 8s (40p) a head, and his dealing days had begun. Having left school during the Second World War at the age of fourteen, Tot immediately began dealing in sheep in a big way. By the time he was twenty-one he had a thriving one-man business and was going to a different market each day of the week. Tot, whose second son now works with him, reckons that well over one hundred thousand sheep pass through his hands every year. In addition to all this, he also lambs a hundred and fifty ewes each spring!

As a child, Tot was no stranger to hard work and helped his father with the family milk round before school. Until 1951 the milk was delivered from a horse and trap, and Tot tells some hair-raising stories of his experiences with the horses in bad weather, when they had to have studs on their shoes to give them a better grip on the snow and ice. Farm horses certainly earned their keep in those days, working long hours in return for their food and a bed at night. During the haymaking season, when working from dawn to dusk, the horses were sometimes so tired that they could barely eat their evening meal, but they would come out fresh after a good night's sleep and give their all again the following day. The men took good care of their horses, washing them down every night with salt water to get rid of the sweat in their coats, and using ointment to massage the horses' tired muscles.

A school holiday job for Tot and his friends was to ride their horses up to Sedbusk, where the shooting parties gathered for the first shoot of the year on the 'glorious twelfth' of August. The grouse shooters would then mount up to ride to the Low Moor, with the lads walking beside them before going on to the next drive. Tot earned the princely sum of 8s (40p) a day for this job, which was good money in those days. As he grew older he saved up to buy himself a bicycle, adding to his income by selling rabbits in the autumn until he had the necessary £4 19s 6d (£4.97½).

Dales pony

In addition to his other farm jobs, Tot used to feed some cows that his father kept in a Mr Dickson's barn. It was near the school, so Mr Dickson would put out some fresh hay the night before and Tot would feed it to the cattle on his way to school each morning. Before school one day, Tot, who was only nine years old at the time, had the fright of his life when he bent down to lift an armful of hay and caught hold of two legs. A voice came out of the depths of the hay saying, 'You needn't be frightened, Tot, it's nobbut me.' When the man sat up, Tot recognized Jack Taylor, the shepherd at Cam Farm with whom Tot was destined to work for a time in later years. It turned out that Jack had had a drop too much to drink the night before and had settled down in the hay for the night, sleeping soundly until disturbed by Tot's arrival.

When Tot and his friends were about twenty they would sometimes, on a Saturday evening, cycle as much as thirty-two miles in a round trip to go to a dance. They would arrive home around three o'clock in the morning, but rarely had the luxury of a lie-in the following day because the animals still had to be fed and tended. Their needs came before those of mere youths craving a few hours of lost sleep.

As with all country folk who work with animals, Tot has a fund of stories to tell about his experiences over the years; every time I see him, he seems to have a new tale to tell. When he was older, Tot worked for a time at Cam Farm, shepherding and herding cattle. One of his jobs was to collect cattle from Hawes station when they arrived there from the local auction marts. Then he would walk them the seven miles back to the farm's grazing land. This entailed taking the beasts right through the town and one day, when the doors of the Conservative Club had unwisely been left open, some of the cattle walked straight in there and got into the pristine billiard room. It was littered with cowpats before Tot could get the animals out again. On another occasion three cows ran into the chemist's shop and blundered about, doing so much damage that Tot and his friend, Bob Stavely, ran away, hoping nobody would realize that they were the ones responsible for the carnage. Of course, the truth came out before long, but they were never charged for all the breakages and mess − much to their relief.

It was not only the cattle which caused problems for Tot: he had trouble when driving sheep through the town, too. He says the most amazing thing he ever saw a sheep do was when one of the fat lambs caught sight of its reflection in a low window in the middle of Hawes and ran at it. It broke the glass and ended up in the sitting room of a house where the occupants were sitting quietly watching television. Tot says he has never been able to decide who was the most surprised by the incident − the sheep, the couple who were in the house, or him.

Many folk in the Dales farming community never take a holiday, and the only time Tot and his wife ever had one was to celebrate their twenty-fifth wedding anniversary. Sheila put her foot down and insisted on marking the event by going on a Caribbean cruise. By the time they returned, Tot was converted to the seagoing life. He told everybody that his time on the high seas had not been long enough after all — but he has never repeated the experiment.

Recently, the shepherd's nightmare visited Tot when he lost one of his dogs. He had left Tip and Scot in his pick-up one morning and it was stolen. The thieves were eventually caught, but Tip was the only dog he got back. Tot was heartbroken, as he had had Scot since buying him as a pup fifteen and a half years before — a marvellous worker and the most faithful dog he has ever had. The loss seems even worse as he has never found out what really happened to the dog, and one is left wondering at the mentality of people who could end the relationship between a man and his old dog in such a heartless fashion.

It is impossible to mention Tot without including his lifelong pal Eddy Iveson, known by the locals as Li'le Eddy. Like Tot, Eddy has lived all his life in the village of Gayle just outside Hawes. But despite their shared surname they are not related — it is just that Iveson is a common name in North Yorkshire. Now only able to walk with the aid of two sticks, Eddy spent his working life as a drover in the Hawes Auction Mart and speaks broad North Yorkshire dialect with a local Hawes accent; it makes any conversation with him a challenge to anybody not from these parts. Eddy has a reputation for continually muttering under his breath, a habit already well developed in his teens when he was overheard as he was walking through the village. 'Swearing like that — you'll never go to heaven!' a woman called Liz Staveley said, to which Eddy replied, 'I don't want to go to heaven — Gayle's good enough for me.'

Li'le Eddy is an enthusiastic supporter of sheepdog trialling and a great admirer of my ex-husband Jim's ability with dogs, demonstrating Jim's runs in the Board Inn at Hawes when he goes there for a pint. He uses matches for the handler, sheep and dog, moving them about appropriately and giving a running commentary. He did the same for my successful *One Man and His Dog* run, to the accompaniment of much ribaldry from his mates in the bar. In 1964 Eddy was already seen as a local personality and George Calvert — another wonderful local character, who founded the Hawes creamery where Wensleydale cheese is made, smoked a clay pipe, and travelled around in a horse and trap with a three-legged dog — wrote a poem in dialect. It really needs to be heard to appreciate it fully, but a verse or two will reveal its flavour and demonstrate how people feel about this hard-working, grand little man.

> *We'a ist et maks the wheels ta go*
> *Fer Annie Mary en her Joe,*
> *Luke's efter't be'as en sarras't coves*
> *Trots up tet syke en than tet shaws.*
> *Li'le Eddy.*

> *We'a ist et maks ther hens ta lay*
> *Beds t'coves wi stre'a en giz em hay*
> *En taks ther be'as tet auction ring,*
> *Wins cards en cups fert prices bring.*
> *Li'le Eddy.*

> *He alis like't a bit a fun*
> *Bet efter o's been said en done*
> *He means ne'a ill, he's good et heart*
> *If ya want a turn he'll dew his part.*
> *Li'le Eddy.*

For the benefit of those not versed in the mysteries of broad Wensleydale, here is what it means (it loses quite a lot in the translation!):

Who is it that makes the wheels go
For Annie Mary and her Joe
Looks after the beasts and feeds the calves
Runs up to the syke [barn] and then to the shaws [outbuildings].
Little Eddy.

Who is that makes the hens to lay
Beds the calves with straw and feeds them hay
And takes their beasts to the auction ring
Wins [prize] cards and cups for the beasts he brings.
Little Eddy.

He always likes a bit of fun
But after all's been said and done
He means no ill, he has a kind heart
If you want a hand he'll do his part.
Little Eddy.

Whenever I drop into the Board Inn, Li'le Eddy calls out to me to join him: 'Coom 'ere, Pet Lamb.' If he wants me to move to left or right, he calls to me in sheepdog terms: 'Come bye, Cropper' or 'Away to me, Cropper'. And then I go over to join him, looking forward to listening to new treasures from his fund of anecdotes and stories.

Then there is Ted Toulan, now in his fifties and shepherding at Troutbeck in the Lake District of Cumbria. A tanned, healthy-looking chap, Ted has a deserved reputation as a good stockman and sheepdog handler, and I first met him at Jim's in Rossendale when he visited Windy Bank to buy young dogs. Every time I saw Ted he was wearing a battered old rabbit-pelt trilby, which I coveted. Eventually I bought myself an Australian bush hat, which was the nearest I could get to it, and I have worn this at work and trials every day since.

Ted left school at the age of fourteen and started to work with sheep the next day. He has been a shepherd ever since, never having wanted to do anything else despite the fact that it was not a well-paid job. Ted once told me: 'I've always thought that men who work with sheep have a sense of humour that's all their own. They need it, too, because the job's hard and they certainly don't do it for the money – there's little of that for the shepherds of this world.'

When he speaks of hard times, Ted relates an incident when one of his daughters was getting married and money was short. 'I got out my only suit. It was the one I'd been married in over twenty years before and, though it still fitted me, it didn't look right. It looked what it was – a demob suit of my uncle's – and my wife wanted me to look my best, so I decided to do something about it. I had a marvellous work dog at the time, so, to please the missus, I sold the dog for £40 and bought myself a nice suit with the proceeds. I looked really smart at the wedding. But a week afterwards, while gathering the hill for clipping, I'd have given four suits just to have had that dog back at my side. Oh, I did miss him!'

In addition to shepherding, Ted had a job as the local gravedigger. One summer night, he had almost finished digging a new grave and was about seven feet down when he heard the click of what turned out to be a camera. Looking up, he saw an American who drawled, 'Hey, man, tell me. Are you digging a grave?' Ted, looking at the man standing amongst the gravestones, dourly replied, 'No. We put t' potatoes in deep round here', and went on with his digging.

As with all shepherds, Ted says that the sheep he can pick out first in a flock are usually the ones which have caused trouble at one time or another. He quotes the instance of the ewe which grazes the roadside on Bank Holiday, getting her lamb killed by a passing car. Then she stops grazing there until next year, when the silly thing will do the same thing again. Steeped in shepherding knowledge and lore, Ted says that, despite the hardships, lack of money and long working hours, he can think of no other life which could have brought him the same satisfaction. 'I've loved the life and met some lovely people in the Lakes and Dales, with rarely a bad 'un amongst them. Good, honest folk who will always help in times of trouble. What more could a man ask for?'

8
MORE ABOUT SHEEPDOGS

I started Max's training after the end of my first lambing at the Fawcetts' farm in Hardraw and he responded well, proving quick to learn and easy to handle. He is a quiet, sensitive dog, with a lot of natural power and feel for the sheep. But after training Royale Moss I was expecting Max to challenge me in the way Moss had done; I decided not to give him the opportunity to do so, and geared his training programme accordingly. He was ready to begin his trialling career in the nurseries at the beginning of the winter of 1988–9. At the first trial he crossed the course – instead of running round the field to get to the far side of the sheep, he ran out a short distance and then changed course to run diagonally across the field between me and the sheep. This meant automatic disqualification, and it was entirely my fault because I failed to set him off properly. Nevertheless he went on to do well by the end of the season: Max gained a place in the first six at most of the trials we went to, including five first places and three seconds.

I was very pleased with myself and my young dog until the following spring, when Richard saw Max running for the first time for several weeks and was horrified. 'What on earth have you done to that dog?' he asked. Suddenly I realized that Max was refusing to walk up after his sheep in the lovely, natural way he had done when he first went out to a flock. He was also hesitating and kept looking back at me for reassurance. The problem was that I had battened down on him too much in his training sessions. I then had to spend several months building up the dog's confidence again, and luckily no permanent damage had been done — by the end of the summer Max was again using his natural sheep sense and work abilities, not looking back, and responding well to my commands; he was also able to use his own initiative when required. All dogs are different, with varying personalities and ability, and it is the handler who must make adjustments to his methods throughout training if he is to enable the dog to reach its full potential.

Max

At five years of age, Max has now developed into a first-class working dog. Like Lad, he has a tremendous ability to balance sheep from any distance and has the same firmness with them, although he is not quite as powerful or good-looking as his uncle. You can see from their pedigrees, reproduced here, that Max and Lad have the same maternal pedigree,

PEDIGREE of LAD

Breed: BORDER COLLIE
Sex: DOG
Colour: BLACK & WHITE - ROUGH - COATED
Date of Birth: 9TH OCTOBER 1980
I.S.D.S. No.: 124750

Owner: KATY CROPPER
Address:
Breeder:
Address:

PARENTS	GRANDPARENTS	GREAT GRANDPARENTS	G. GREAT GRANDPARENTS	G. G. GREAT GRANDPARENTS
SIRE DILWYN LAD J.R.THOMAS I.S.D.S. Reg. No. 100895	SIRE CRAIG J.R.THOMAS I.S.D.S. 59425	CHIP 29946 L.R.SUTER	BILL 16633 D.W.EVANS	MOSS 4975 H.G.NORTHERTON / FLOSS 5582 H.G.NORTHERTON
			MEG 19713 A.H.WILLIAMS	ROY 14602 J.H.BARKER / MEG 16167 T.H.BAKER
		JILL 49652 H.G.HANNAN	GARRY 19382 A.CHAPMAN	CAP 7554 J.WALKER / NELL 15588 J.MARK
			JESS 37142 H.G.HANNAN	CHIP 29944 H.G.HANNAN / NELL 23225 H.G.HANNAN
	DAM BET H.G.J.HAVARD I.S.D.S. 66184	JIM 47244 S.B.PRICE	WISTON CAP 31154 J.RICHARDSON	CAP 15834 J.RICHARDSON / FLY 2500 N.C.HETHERINGTON
			KATY 20820 T.MURRAY	LAD 12476 / CLUSS 14756 T.M.PANTON
		JESS 57876 H.G.HANNENS	MOSS 41957 R.H.HINDLE	BROKEN ABBEE 24634 N.G.CHAPMAN / FLY 34035
			MEG 48977 R.K.NICHOLLS	ROY 15593 A.JONES / NELL 20471 A.JONES
DAM FLOSS J.HAWKINS I.S.D.S. Reg. No. 88122	SIRE FLEET J.CROPPER I.S.D.S. 38813	ROCK 27425 J.H.T.BATHGATE	HOPE 13418 R.H.HARDIE	HOPE 7029 F.ANDERSON / TIB 8658 M.FALCONER
			MIST 14246 A.D.R.CROCKBEIN	TWEED 9601 J.M.WILSON / BEN 7553 A.D.R.CROCKBEIN
		TRIM 26864 J.BONELLA	BILL II 17937 T.K.WILSON	WHITEHOPE NAP 5685 T.H.WILSON / MEG 12730 T.K.WILSON
			TIB 21675 J.BONELLA	JAN 13223 W.BELL / TRIM 13771 J.M.DURNAN
	DAM HOPE J.HAWKINS I.S.D.S. 73538	MIRK 28776 J.NETTRICK	CAP 13274 W.N.COOK	CAP 10680 M.COLLEY / LASSIE 10680 M.W.COOK
			GAEL 14463 T.M.KNIGHT	WHITEHOPE NAP 8685 T.M.WILSON / DOT 11225 T.T.MCKNIGHT
		GAEL 57306 J.HAWKINS	SPOT 24981 J.GILCRIST	BOB 12684 J.GILCHRIST / WISTON NANTY 9596 PHIL.HEBDON
			DOT 51922 J.HAWKINS	GLEN 16214 W.D.GLEN / DOT 25586 G.H.WESTON

I certify that this pedigree is correct to the best of my knowledge. Signed.................... Date..........

Published by Working Sheepdog News, Ty'n-y-Caeau, Pwll Glas, Ruthin, Clwyd, North Wales LL15 2LT. U.K. Telephone: 08245 394

Lad's Pedigree

PEDIGREE of MAX

Breed: BORDER COLLIE
Sex: DOG
Colour: BLACK AND WHITE ROUGH - COATED
Date of Birth: 28TH NOVEMBER 1986
I.S.D.S. No.: 166230

Owner: KATY CROPPER
Address:
Breeder:
Address:

PARENTS	GRANDPARENTS	GREAT GRANDPARENTS	G. GREAT GRANDPARENTS	G. G. GREAT GRANDPARENTS
SIRE CAP J.T.STAMFERS I.S.D.S. Reg. No. 104643	SIRE BEN A.H.HEATON I.S.D.S. 86925	MICK 76551 A.G.HEATON	BEN 56646 D.INSTER	WISTON CAP 31154 J.RICHARDSON / BESS 29525 D.RUSSELL
			SHELL 56986 J.R.ROBINSON	BEN 41463 R.DALEY / NELL 48753 A.MAY
		LADY 80173 A.G.HEATON	SPOT 59638 A.HEATON	MIRK 35066 J.NORTON / NELL 50748 J.H.T.BATHGATE
			LYN 66008 A.H.HEATON	LADDIE 24112 A.G.HEATON / DINAH 55846 R.J.NICHOLLS
	DAM MOONRAKER RONA J.T.STAMMERS I.S.D.S. 87893	LITCH 70955 F.W.SAUNER	GLEN 47241 T.MURRAY	WISTON CAP 31154 J.RICHARDSON / KATY 20820 T.MURRAY
			KYP 47075 T.J.S.COGGAN	SPOT 32668 G.S.MCLLARNEY / FLY 30724 C.D.BARRON
		QUEEN 73877 F.W.SAUNER	JAN 65384 T.A.W.COGGAN	TWEED 24608 T.A.COGGAN / MAID 58718 W.S.HETHERINGTON
			CREE 58432 T.J.S.COGGAN	WISTON CAP 31154 J.RICHARDSON / CREE 50806 A.B.CASE
DAM BESS J.T.STAMMERS I.S.D.S. Reg. No. 124749	SIRE DILWYN LAD II J.R.THOMAS I.S.D.S. 100895	CRAIG 59425 J.R.THOMAS	CHIP 29946 L.R.SUTER	BILL 16633 D.W.EVANS / MEG 19713 A.H.WILLIAMS
			JILL 49652 H.G.HANNAN	GARRY 19382 A.CHAPMAN / JESS 37142 H.G.HANNAN
		BET 66184 H.G.J.HAVARD	JIM 47244 S.B.PRICE	WISTON CAP 31154 J.RICHARDSON / KATY 20820 T.MURRAY
			JESS 57876 H.G.J.HAVARD	MOSS 41957 R.H.NICHOLLS / NELL 48977 R.K.NICHOLLS
	DAM FLOSS J.HAWKINS I.S.D.S. 88122	FLEET 38813 J.CROPPER	ROCK 27425 J.H.T.BATHGATE	HOPE 13418 A.D.R.CROCKBEIN / MIST 14246
			TRIM 26864 J.BONELLA	BILL II 17937 T.H.WILSON / TIB 21675 J.BONELLA
		WYNCHNOR HOPE 73538 J.HAWKINS	MIRK 28776 J.C.NETTRICK	CAP 13274 M.W.COOK / GAEL 14463 T.T.MCKNIGHT
			GAEL 57306 A.HENLY	SPOT 24981 J.GILCRIST / DOT 51922 J.HAWKINS

I certify that this pedigree is correct to the best of my knowledge. Signed.................... Date..........

Published by Working Sheepdog News, Ty'n-y-Caeau, Pwll Glas, Ruthin, Clwyd, North Wales LL15 2LT. U.K. Telephone: 08245 394

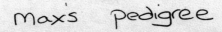

Max's Pedigree

but Max has so far sired good progeny from whatever bitch is used in the mating and all his pups have gone on to make good working sheepdogs and some trials dogs. Sadly, no litters have resulted from any of Lad's matings over the past years and, now that he is nearly twelve, it seems that I will never have the pleasure of training one of his offspring and no dog to carry on his full line. But life with these dogs is full of disappointments, as well as pleasures and triumphs; it is one of the things which make it all so interesting (and frustrating at times), and is the reason why successful handlers never stop learning, questioning and adjusting.

One thing which really pleased me during that first year at Hardraw was the fact that, whenever I met Jim on the trials field, we were able to bury our differences and gradually build up a friendship based on mutual liking and shared interests, but without the emotional involvement which had proved our undoing. To this day, he continues to encourage me with my dogs and I value his criticism and advice as much as ever. He is one of the best sheepdog handlers in the country, as well as a great personality and a valued friend.

During the months when I was training Max, Trim was continuing to develop her skills and was doing well in her first Open trials season. I was also still running Lad at trials, where he was giving a good account of himself and astonishing spectators with his sheer guts and personality. However, by the end of 1988 I had noticed that, after big trials with a punishing outrun, particularly over hilly ground, Lad was beginning to get rather tired. So I decided to retire him from trials and heavy work at the end of the year in the knowledge that he would still be able to enjoy working in the demonstrations at shows which had booked me for the following summer. Even so, he had had an illustrious trials career up to the age of eight, which was quite an achievement, and he was retired from that scene before his loss of physical stamina could cause deterioration in his work. By comparison, demonstrations take place in a more enclosed space and are far less arduous — ideal for a dog who still loves to work but has limitations imposed by a combination of physical disability and increasing age.

I started demonstrating with sheepdogs after a telephone call from Jim, who asked me if I would stand in for him at a small agricultural show because he was ill and therefore unable to do it himself. Although

I felt nervous when I first went into the ring, I soon relaxed and found myself enjoying the chance to show the public how clever these dogs are in their handling of sheep. After that first appearance I was invited to repeat the performance at other small shows in the same year, and in the last couple of years we have graduated to appearing at the big three-day events; there I have made many new friends among the show people working regularly on the circuit.

At first I did a fairly simple demonstration, which outlined the different manoeuvres required in the handling of a small flock of sheep, and the commentaries were done for me by professionals. But it was not long before I began to add more variety and pace in order to give additional interest for the spectators. I decided to use Trim for the serious part of the performance when working sheep, and bought six white Aylesbury ducks to provide a contrast. When Lad first saw the ducks he immediately rounded them up as he would a flock of sheep, and since that time he has looked upon them as his own personal charges. A friend made me some little yellow gates, and later I acquired a tunnel (like the ones they use in agility trials for dogs), a small chute and a large children's paddling pool. The idea was that Lad would round up the ducks, get them to walk between the gates, then herd them into the tunnel before coercing them up the chute. The ducks would then slide down in turn into the water, and that would end the show.

Lad always causes a stir at the shows when I bring out the ducks. Having started off with the big white Aylesburys, I later added a black one named Leroy whom I introduce as the new recruit to the team. Leroy has a mind of his own and refuses to conform to the behaviour required of him; he always wanders off by himself, refusing to go up the slide with the others, and as a result the spectators love him. However, Lad usually manages to maintain reasonable order – although he too can behave unpredictably at times. One of his favourite games in the show ring (and he always takes me by surprise when he does this) is to get the ducks into the long tunnel and then follow them into it, running through and emerging at the far end, covered in feathers, before the ducks reach it. He looks round for the applause and then, as soon as the ducks begin to appear, shoos them back into the tunnel and they have to retrace their steps. In hot weather, after the ducks have gone down the shute into the pool, Lad brings the house down when he jumps in with them, lying full length to cool himself down, to the accompaniment of much quacking and squawking. Not surprisingly, my friends are beginning to think that I have developed a duck fetish. Not only do I have seven ducks for demonstration purposes, but I also have a large variety of plastic ducks in the bathroom (seventy-two to date) and a duck telephone, which quacks instead of ringing in the way of the phones of more sensible people.

When I was planning my demonstrations, I had to do some serious thinking. I wanted to avoid turning them into a circus act because I felt that this would denigrate the beauty and skill of the working Border Collie, but I did want to make our time in the ring enjoyable and interesting for the many people who had never watched a sheepdog trial in their lives. So I decided to make the demonstration half educational and half amusement, and it has proved to be a combination which has worked well. It has also done a good public relations job for the Border Collie and his world.

I also knew that I was going to have to do a balancing act with my dogs. Lad was no problem because he was now retired from work and trialling, but I did not want to do anything which would spoil either Trim's or Max's performance in the serious business of shepherding work and trials. On the other hand I had to make a living and, although the dog training was going well, it was not bringing in enough money for me to be financially secure. With the money I could earn on the show circuit this matter would be remedied, and I would be doing work where I could keep my dogs with me. I made the decision to carry on using my dogs in demonstrations with a proviso that, if any of them showed signs of going off in their work or trials performance as a result, I would take them out of the show.

In 1990, both Trim and Max qualified at the English National to compete in the International Sheep Dog Trials, which were held in September at Alnwick Castle in Northumberland. Trim's run was not up to her usual standard, probably because I was drawn for the very first run of the trials and was rather apprehensive, not having had the advantage of watching other runs. But Max's run was a different matter – by the time we reached the pen, we were having the best run of the day so far. I was delighted with Max's performance and knew that, if we could pen the sheep without too much trouble, we had a chance of being in the final run-off for the Supreme Championship on the Saturday. But it was not to be: we just failed to get the sheep into the pen, which meant that we could not attempt the single – separating one animal from the rest of the small flock – to finish the run. By this time too many points had been lost to keep us in the competition, but my dog had worked well and that was sufficient reward for me.

During the following winter, Max began to show signs of loss of confidence when trialling. When I discussed the problem with Richard, he said he thought that, by running Max to demonstrate brace work with Trim at the shows, I was spoiling him for working single-handed. He said Max was getting confused, and as a result was no longer sure of himself on the trials field. I was in full agreement, so I have had to make the decision to restrict Max to shepherding and trials. He is now in his prime and has many more years in which to make his mark in the trialling world, while I have other dogs coming up to take his place in the demonstration team.

Fortunately, Trim seems to be equally happy whatever work she is doing – I can run her in a demonstration and on the way home enter her for an evening run at a trial. She will immediately adapt to the new situation, knowing exactly what to do and then doing it well. This all underlines how individual dogs differ and how watchful you need to be as a handler at all times to avoid making too many mistakes. I am sure that Max will soon settle back into a normal work routine – the next lambing season will help. Then he should go back to competing in sheepdog trials with renewed confidence.

When I began to train my first sheepdog in Anglesey, I had already learnt some of the basics of animal training from my time with horses when preparing them for dressage and three-day eventing. I knew that good communication is all-important to successful training, while the continual handling, grooming, cleaning and feeding entailed in their general care helps build up a good relationship – essential to the trainer, and to the animal if its confidence is to grow. Another important attribute is to understand what is going on inside an animal's head: some of this comes from continually working with the animal, some can be learnt from observation and experience during training sessions, and some comes from being able to think flexibly and with imagination – I suppose you could call this lateral thinking. Most importantly, an animal's reasoning powers are different from our own, and we must make allowances for this.

There is no doubt that I was always too soft with my animals at first, allowing them to take liberties which diminished my position as leader of the pack (an essential to successful dog training) and letting them feel they were the boss, rather than the other way round. As time went on, and particularly after entering the sheepdog world, I learned that firm, consistent handling (not to be confused with undue harshness, punishment or brutality) will lead to a happier, responsive and well-behaved animal which is a pleasure to have around. This is because both trainer and trained know their boundaries and have a desire to respond to one another based on mutual trust, respect and liking.

In my experience, for the trainer learning never stops – if it does, he will become increasingly inflexible in his approach to the task. By this, I do not mean one should change one's approach to a particular problem just for the hell of it; rather that two heads are sometimes better than one and, by exchanging ideas and experiences, trainers can continue to add to their own store of knowledge, filing away things in their minds which they think might be of use to them and rejecting anything with which they fail to agree. When first training my dogs I was avid for information, accepting everything said to me as being 'right' and not questioning an experienced handler's approach to the task – and this was as it should be, because I had to have a starting point if I was not to fall by the wayside. However, as my own experience developed I began to understand that what might work for one handler would not necessarily be a suitable approach for another. After all, since every dog and every handler are different there must inevitably be variations in approach and attitude. And so, as time went on, I learned to listen, digest, keep or discard as I thought fit, and all the time my basic knowledge was increasing.

While I was with Jim I accepted his advice about the need to be firm with my dogs and to make my approach to them more consistent and quietly authoritative – training wisdom of the highest order. However, I could not agree with him that a sheepdog should never live in the house if it was to be any good on the trials field. Since I have been on my own again Lad and Trim have been at my side, day and night, indoors and out, and I challenge anybody to say that it has damaged their performance when working — in fact, I think the closeness of the relationship has enhanced my working partnership with them both. I hasten to add that I agree with Jim up to a point; both Trim and Lad were fully trained before becoming house dogs and, although I sometimes have youngsters in the house in the daytime before their serious work training begins, the minute they begin to work with the sheep they live outside in their own kennels until they are fully trained. By doing so they seem to concentrate better on the task of working, learning, resting and giving some thought to what they have been doing on the training field. For Jim, his method works; and for me, my method works. So who is right? The answer is that both systems are right, because they work for the individuals using them.

A good dog handler must have the confidence to relax under pressure, always remembering that the dog is relying on being handled quietly, calmly and with understanding — skills which can fly out of the window in competitive or dangerous situations. Because I train working sheepdogs for shepherding, sheepdog trialling and demonstrations, I tend to look at my approach to the task from that angle. But I know that much of what I am saying here applies equally to those who train dogs to the gun, for agility, for working trials, for the show bench or as actors for stage and screen. Pet owners who want to have well-behaved, happy dogs in their homes can learn much from professional dog trainers, because the basics of training are always alike. It is when specialized work training begins that requirements diverge, as will the age at which this starts.

With the exception of Lad, who is in a class of his own, I have found that having a dog from the time it is a puppy helps to develop a better bond with it and (an important factor) I know exactly what has happened to each puppy during his most formative months. Bad early experiences such as a lack of socialization and learning situations, inconsistent handling or, as sometimes happens, outright cruelty, can have a lasting effect on a dog's personality. They may lead to learning or concentration difficulties and irrational behaviour — these will affect the dog's responses to training, and, of course, his reaction to human beings. I have also found that it is far better to have just one or two starter youngsters at a time. Some trainers like to start off whole litters when they reach a trainable age and then pick out the most promising young dogs before selling the rest, but this system does not work for me — I tend to make a commitment to a smaller number and then do my best to enable them to realize their full potential over the next year or so.

There is one mistake which is easy to make when you find yourself with an intelligent youngster who is keen, willing and eager to learn. Your excitement mounts because you know you have a promising dog which could take you both to the top if you can help him develop his full potential, so you concentrate on his training, start far too early — and then overdo it. Anybody who has trained sheepdogs for work and trials will have experienced this. I remember seeing a keen four-month-old dog demonstrating considerable interest in sheep and moving in a classy way with just a little eye, a natural cast and lovely balance. His owner was delighted with the dog, and I could barely believe my eyes when he kept it out with the sheep for a whole hour! Not surprisingly, the pup eventually became bored and confused, going off to sniff at tussocks of grass. The handler began to run the dog in nursery trials at the end of the year, and it was sad to watch the animal because it had lost heart, had a slow, disinterested outrun and was unable to concentrate on the task in hand.

One area in which I am always very careful is the dogs' vaccination programme — the effect of the lesson I learned from Sheila Grew all those years ago. I carefully note in my diary every year when each dog's booster vaccination is due, and it is a job which I never delay. Any litters of puppies are vaccinated against the killer parvovirus infection at around seven weeks; then, if they are still with me, they receive routine prophylactic injections at ten and twelve weeks. My vet also gives another parvo injection at seven months. When new owners take their puppies away — usually when they are between eight and ten weeks old — I always advise them to get their animals vaccinated appropriately, warn them of the dangers in not doing so, and then pray that they will follow my advice — or at least consult their vet on suitable times for injection, as these can vary according to the vaccine used.

I also take precautions with any bitch I use for breeding purposes. If she has had her booster within six months of being put to the dog, she should have sufficient antibodies in her bloodstream to protect her pups

The family at Gloddaeth Hall near Llandudno, North Wales around 1968. I'm on the far right.

My beloved Trish, the matron at St David's College, founded by my father.

With my first pony, Peter Pan.
Jean Lomas

LEFT: At the Royal Lancashire Show with my former husband, Jim Cropper and our dogs; from the left: Tyne, Royale Moss, Lad, Cap and Fonzi.

BELOW: Working with Lad and Trim in the Yorkshire Dales above Hardraw. *Roger Scruton*

LEFT: Mike Csernovits with Mick in 1978.

BELOW: At Windy Bank Farm in Rossendale, Yorkshire with the dogs: Lad (front left), Hattie (behind Lad), Trim, Queenie and Royale Moss. *Nick Clarke*

ABOVE: Moving sheep on Richard's farm. *Richard Fawcett*

LEFT: Ted Toulan working at The Croft, Hardraw. *Richard Fawcett*

BELOW: A great Dales character, the incomparable Li'le Eddy.

ABOVE: Jack and Dick hand-shearing. *Richard Fawcett*

RIGHT: I have learnt so much from my friend, Sheila Ellis's lifetime experience of working dogs.

BELOW: My brave friend, Susie Baker.

RIGHT: The new lambs and their mothers on the road to Hardraw. *Roger Scruton*

BELOW: At the back of my home, Lilac Cottage, with Trim and my Aylesbury ducks – Mavis, Andrea, Sandra, Clara, Kate and Freda. *Stuart Mason, Sunday Express*

LEFT: Future champions! *Richard Fawcett*

BOTTOM LEFT: A good lambing dog.

BELOW: With the Duchess of Devonshire, after winning *One Man and His Dog*. On my right is H. Glyn Jones who won the Brace championship.

ABOVE: An intimate
moment with Trim at Lilac
Cottage. *Sunday Express*

RIGHT: The puppies at the
barn door. *Roger Scruton*

up to the time they are vaccinated themselves. However, if the time lapse is over six months, I take her for a booster before putting her to the dog. One other measure I take is never to allow unvaccinated dogs into my kennels for training — I always ask the owners for proof of vaccination before the dog's arrival. A spin-off from setting high standards is that they may rub off on to those who have not given sufficient thought to these things in the past — a way of teaching dog care without ramming it down people's throats.

Canine parvovirus is a worldwide disease which first appeared in the United Kingdom in 1978 and reached epidemic proportions in the following two years, killing many previously healthy animals and causing havoc among litters of puppies, which are especially susceptible. After vigorous research vets are now able to inject reliable, safe vaccines which keep the spread of the disease in check — but of course any vaccine relies on the willingness of owners to recognize the danger and take their animals to the vet for regular booster doses.

People who have witnessed the suffering, pain and distress caused by parvovirus find it a truly horrific experience. After an incubation period of only a few days the initial symptoms are lethargy, loss of appetite and a sharply raised temperature. These are followed by extremely severe, bloodstained diarrhoea and rapid dehydration. Few dogs, in particular puppies, can survive this, and death ensues in a matter of days. There is a second, rarer form of the disease which causes inflammation of the heart muscle in very young puppies. The permanent damage which results may kill them months or even years later. But if the mother has been vaccinated, her antibodies will protect the puppies at this crucial stage in their lives.

I have been surprised recently to meet several pet dog owners who had never heard of parvovirus, and it is worrying to find that ignorance of this kind still exists because it can lead to unnecessary suffering. Even with a full understanding of the infectious diseases which can affect and kill dogs, tragedies still happen and we can be taken unawares; but at least the possibility can be minimized if adequate care is taken. Part of the problem is the tenacity of parvovirus — it can still be *carried* by vaccinated dogs, which excrete it in their faeces where it may lie dormant for months, or even years, before finding a susceptible, unvaccinated dog.

It may seem unnecessary to point out the care needed if bitches in season are not to be mated accidentally by any dogs on the premises, but it is surprising how many of us make mistakes. Normally, as soon as I find that a bitch is coming into season I keep her away from the dogs at all times, firmly at my side when I have her out and otherwise in the house or kennel where she can get up to no mischief. However, nature being what it is, even those of us who preach good management should never become complacent because we can still be caught out, as I was in the winter of 1991.

Dog safely in Kennel

Although Trim was in season, I felt it was safe to leave her loose in the yard for a few minutes while I put on my coat and boots. Then the telephone rang (or, more correctly, quacked), and by the time I went out to get her ten minutes had gone by and she was nowhere to be seen. As soon as I called her she came running back from the village and I put her into her kennel, oblivious to the fact that she had been consorting with

Winston, a lovely English Setter who has quite a reputation with the ladies. Three hours later, when I returned from working on Dodd Fell, I discovered that Ruby and Roy Norris, Winston's owners, were getting frantic because they had been trying to contact me to let me know that Winston had mated with Trim that morning. Apparently Roy had had Winston on one of those long, expanding leads, and when the dog saw Trim he just took off, dragging Roy behind him as he followed Trim round the corner and to the village green. Trim ran up to Winston, flirting outrageously while Roy tried to keep himself upright on the icy road. He had failed to keep the dogs apart because he was skidding about so much, and nature had taken its course.

I thanked Roy for letting me know the worst and leaped into the pick-up, with Trim sitting on the seat next to me looking virginal and unconcerned as we drove to the veterinary surgery for the culprit to be injected against conception. When I told the vet that Trim had been mated by an English Setter, he laughed and asked, 'It wasn't Winston, was it?' so Trim was obviously not his first love. I had a nail-biting few weeks until it became apparent that she had not conceived. Needless to say, the whole farming community soon heard what had happened and were quite merciless with me. Richard said he was going to put an advertisement in the paper saying: 'Pups for sale out of 1990 *One Man and His Dog* champion and sired by beautiful English Setter', while sheepdog handlers at the trials were asking me what my nursery dog for the winter would look like, warming to their theme and giving their opinion of the various weird and wonderful characteristics and attributes which could be expected from a Border Collie/English Setter cross-bred. They had a field day!

I am convinced that eyesight in dogs can differ, as can their hearing, and this will affect their responses. Some dogs seem to hear well from far away, no matter how windy or stormy it may be, while others get a bit confused until they are near enough to the handler to hear the commands or whistles. This is not necessarily because these dogs are easier to control close to hand, but because they simply cannot hear so well against a lot of background noise. For instance, Trim can hear me in any weather and at great distances while Max's hearing is less acute, so I have to make allowances for this when working in bad weather. There is no doubt that some dogs listen better than others –

and some dogs may be concentrating so much on the sheep that they simply ignore the commands. These are all factors which have to be borne in mind by the trainer.

Before any puppy is brought home and training begins, the owner must think about housing, feeding, grooming, affection, veterinary care and, not least, the amount of time available to the handler to deal with these needs. Unless there is going to be somebody at home during the daytime to attend to a puppy's requirements, perhaps it is not the right time to acquire him. To shut a puppy away day after day for hours on end, with company for only a couple of hours in the evening and even less in the mornings, is nothing short of cruel. Would-be owners should always think of the dog's needs before their own, and act accordingly.

While I can now always remain calm and quiet during training sessions, there are still times during competition at major trials when I am more likely to go haywire — usually if I am not feeling 100 per cent for some reason, or am particularly tense, as I was during the semi-final run for *One Man and His Dog*. So this is the area on which I have to concentrate all the time. I always go out to the post wanting to win, but the flow of adrenalin has to be controlled if the dog and sheep are to sense this and move more quietly. If I am tense and shouting, dog and sheep respond accordingly and I get nowhere.

Sometimes, people comment that I was lucky because I had good sheep for my run, but most of the time I am convinced that they were quiet because I kept calm and unruffled, the dog moved in a careful, controlled manner and the sheep responded quietly. I know that all handlers get terrible, unpredictable sheep from time to time at trials; but I am prepared to stick my neck out and say that, if they are like that, nine times out of ten it is the handler's fault. I sometimes demonstrate this point in the show ring when talking about the way dogs work with sheep, and the importance of the handler. It is very easy to do — absolute chaos one minute, with dog and sheep all over the place, and then, after I quieten things down, a steady dog and orderly sheep moving wherever they are supposed to go.

Watch any handler who achieves a nice, controlled run and similar remarks about good sheep will be made. But I have seen handlers like Jim who seem able to put a spell on the sheep, never mind the dog!

Often Jim will have a perfect run when the one before his and the one immediately after were impossible — it happens too often to be luck every time. Of course, if somebody is unlucky enough to get one crazy Swaledale ewe in his packet of sheep (they are easy to spot because they come out with their heads stuck up in the air), there is no way he will be able to control what happens and the run has to be put down to experience.

This quietness of approach with dogs should start right at the beginning, ideally from the time they are born. I use an unhurried approach to them at all times, keeping my voice as quiet as possible. Then, when they have done something wrong and I need to let them know about it, all I have to do is speak just slightly louder, slightly more urgently. Or I will growl at them quietly, and they know immediately that I am not pleased with them. I have found that the growl has more effect than anything else and they always dislike it — this applies equally to puppies and fully grown dogs. If you think about it, this approach makes sound sense. If I use a loud, harsh voice all the time, the dog will tend to respond in a rough, harsh way. Then, when it does go wrong, I will have to shout loudly to get it to take notice. With the softer type of dog this might have the effect of cowing it, while the harder type of dog will just get increasingly defiant. By always speaking quietly to my dogs I avoid introducing tension and anxiety into them — and the formation of a vicious circle of conditioned responses which will affect all their future behaviour.

Tension can be introduced in various ways, some of them quite cruel, although the perpetrators of this kind of thing feel that they are doing the only thing possible if they are to keep their dog under control. One man brought his dog to me after asking if I would be interested in buying it, adding that it was uncontrollable and kept rushing to grip the sheep. When he arrived, I could hardly believe my eyes — there was a huge choke chain around the dog's neck, and a loop of it was also clipped round his lower jaw to give the man more control. The chain was attached to a rope which would have held the weight of a mountaineer, and the man carried a thick stick. We went out to the field and I said, 'Let me see him run, then.' After he had warned me that the dog might damage the sheep the man removed the rope, leaving the choke chain in place, and sent the dog off. He shouted at the top of his voice as it ran straight through the middle of the sheep and scattered them in all directions. The dog continued to rush wildly around the field, with the man bellowing ineffectually, until it reluctantly returned to its owner.

'Here, let me have a go,' I said. As soon as he returned I knelt down in front of the dog to remove the chain. Stroking the dog and talking to him quietly, I could see that he had good, dark eyes and an honest sort of face, and he looked me in the eyes. I thought he seemed a grand dog and warmed to him immediately. After spending a little time reassuring him, I got to my feet, saying, 'Come bye' very quietly. And then he was off, steady as you like, to run round to the back of his sheep — a bit tightly, but at least he had not gone through the middle of them this time, and everything was under control. He settled down at the back of the sheep and I just let him bring them to me, not saying a word. Then I moved about to keep the sheep walking, with the dog following them and moving himself side to side on the far side of them to balance the sheep and hold them up to me — in other words, to keep them close to me. I bought that dog and he is turning out to be a real cracker — no sign of gripping at all. I am sure this is because the tension and stress have been removed and the dog can relax. He is proving very promising and is responding well to his training, so it is going to be interesting to watch his future development.

9

STARTING
TO TRAIN
A PUPPY

CHOOSING THE RAW MATERIAL

I always feel that the training of my own dogs begins with the choice of puppy — and even before that, as I follow certain basic rules before going to the breeder to make my selection. These rules are:

(a) both parents must be proven working and trials dogs;

(b) the sire and dam must both be registered with the International Sheepdog Society (ISDS);

(c) the sire and dam must both have been eye-tested and certified free of the two commonest genetic eye disorders in the Border Collie — Collie eye anomaly (CEA) and progressive retinal atrophy (PRA);

(d) if the parents are not known to me, I make an appointment to see them working before I look at the litter. At the same time, I ask for the registered names and numbers of the puppies' parents in order to be able to check their lines back over several generations. Now that I am more experienced I know the breed lines I prefer, so I tend to make up my own mind these days, although an additional opinion is always useful.

Having made an appointment to see a litter of puppies I do my best to arrive on time, making sure that I am suitably dressed for walking across muddy yards and fields, coping with bad weather and going down on my knees to handle the pups and play with them. Part of my preparation is to scrub my boots thoroughly before going — this lessens the risk of taking infection into the whelping area. I also wash my hands before handling the pups — shades of Sheila Grew again! I take money with me (cheque or cash, as agreed beforehand with the vendor) to pay for my potential purchase, and a cage or box lined with newspaper in which to put the pup to take it home. Often, a friend will come with me and have the puppy on her (newspaper-covered) lap during the journey, with some old towelling to hand just in case. This is probably the best method, because she can handle and talk to the pup to reassure it in the strange, noisy surroundings of the car while I keep my mind on the road. It is better not to give a puppy food if it is going to travel, which can usually be arranged beforehand with the breeder. This can save an unpleasant mess in the car and, more importantly, can also save the puppy a lot of stress.

MAKING UP MY MIND

When confronted with a litter of sound, healthy, boisterous puppies, with little to choose between them, I will go for the one whose appearance and demeanour please me most — this does not mean that I have chosen the 'best' puppy, merely the one which appeals to me. This is important, as I must have an instinctive liking for any dog I train and this provides as good a start as any.

Once that decision has been made, I look at the pup's teeth to ensure that the jaw is correctly set (neither under- nor over-shot), and I also like to see a black roof to his mouth — nothing to do with the quality of a dog, but for some reason I like it. My feelings about ear carriage are also based on a personal aesthetic preference. I dislike floppy ears in a Border Collie and look for a pup whose ears show signs of being held up on the head, indicating that when he is an adult he will be either prick-eared, or have upright ears which just turn over at the tips. Then I check to see that any dew claws have been removed — if they have not, as the pup grows these useless claws also grow larger and can get caught up in undergrowth and brambles, resulting in injury, pain and infection. Removing dew claws is a simple procedure if done in the first week of life, but after that time requires a general anaesthetic and surgery — all at extra expense to me and discomfort to the dog. I watch him running around to see that his hocks are nice and straight and check his tummy for hernia — a fairly common problem in pups, which often needs surgery to repair. Then, providing the puppy is sound, I make the deal.

Sheepdog puppies

At the time of writing, a good eight-week-old Border Collie puppy from working lines will cost something between £70 and £150, depending on its breeding lines, its parents' working ability and their successes at sheepdog trials. Why the puppies should be valued so much lower than those of other breeds, which can sell for several hundred pounds, is something I can never understand when I think of the supreme ability and intelligence of working sheepdogs.

HELPING THE PUPPY TO SETTLE

Before leaving with my puppy, I ask about his feeding routine and the type of food used, the last time he was wormed, and his date of birth. I then tell the breeder what name I would like the pup registered under — he will include this information, and my name and address as the owner, when he registers the litter. If the litter has already been registered, a transfer form is completed to register me as the new owner with the ISDS.

The International Sheepdog Society registration of puppies is somewhat different from that of the Kennel Club in that long, fanciful names are not allowed to be used for registration under any circumstances. All names must be short — preferably one syllable, two at most — and suitable for use when commanding on the field. Thus the everyday names such as Cap, Trim and Lad are the actual names under which the dogs are registered in the stud book. The only deviation from this is when the breeder has paid a fee to register a breeding prefix with the Society; but even prefixes have to be short and sensible. Inevitably this system leads to continual repetition of names in the stud book as there are only a certain number which are suitable. In the sheepdog trialling world, dogs with the same name are identified by using the name of the handler — Glyn Jones's Taff, Jim Cropper's Cap, Katy Cropper's Trim and so on. The name chosen for registration can be taken from one of the puppy's forebears, but is often a name for which the new owner has a particular preference. For instance the handler Alan Jones always has a dog called Roy; whenever his existing one dies, the next male pup he gets will always be registered as Roy!

At first I will feed my new puppy in whatever way the breeder has been doing, gradually changing over to my own preferred diet over the next couple of weeks — this helps to avoid any unnecessary digestive disturbances and upsets, which can set a pup back. Until the puppy's vaccination programme is completed I keep him away from the other dogs; he only runs around in his own kennel and run, or in the kitchen. Two weeks after the last injection — usually around the age of twelve weeks — the puppy can be allowed to associate with the other dogs and have free run of the place when I am there with him.

I now tend to buy two pups at a time and house them together because I have found they thrive well this way — they have one another's company, which gives them a lot of exercise together, and they learn to take the rough and tumble of life in the months before training begins — although pups on their own can do equally well if given plenty of attention, affection and exercise. By the time they reach four months of age I tend to separate the pups and put them in their own individual kennels, which stand next to each other.

KEEPING THE PUPPY IN GOOD CONDITION, AND GETTING TO KNOW EACH OTHER

In addition to handling, feeding and housing the pup, I worm him regularly with a product recommended by the vet, de-flea him routinely and regularly check for abrasions, sores and bald patches – this enables me to nip any small problems in the bud to ensure the pup keeps in good condition. I also spend as much time as I can with a new puppy, getting to know him, handling and grooming him, giving him a lot of affection and generally enjoying him as he settles into his new routine and he in turn gets to know me. This is a time which I always enjoy and the puppies soon begin to look for affection and human contact – something which will come in useful when training begins.

GETTING USED TO A VEHICLE

With vaccinations completed, I begin to educate the puppy in matters which will stand him in good stead as he grows older, and on which we can both build as he becomes more mature. Other than that first journey which cannot be avoided, I introduce him to a vehicle very gradually. First, I put him in the back of the pick-up for a few seconds only, often with another, trained dog in there for company. Then, over the next few days, I gradually lengthen the time he is left in there, but still keep an eye on him. Later, this is followed by starting the engine up, and then stopping it before removing the puppy – this helps him to get used to the sound and vibration. Eventually I take him on very short journeys of only a mile or so, slowly lengthening them as the puppy grows accustomed to the movement.

After every journey with a youngster I avoid taking him from the vehicle immediately – this ensures that he gets used to waiting to be let out and he learns to be patient. If the pup tries to bark or whine before being let out, I growl quietly at him, then remove him as soon as he stops. By taking things slowly and steadily in this way, I have never yet had a dog which would not travel happily in a vehicle. Neither has any dog of mine ever been travel-sick or yapped continually to be let out.

SOCIALIZING THE PUPPY

As the puppy grows more used to travelling I can take him with me everywhere I go, increasing our mutual contact and introducing him to a wide variety of situations and people to help him become well socialized. I also have my pups outside in the garden as much as possible – this helps them to get plenty of exercise, to develop their muscles, their brains, their curiosity and their stamina. When visitors arrive, I encourage them to handle and talk to the pups to increase their human contacts. I also take the pups walking in the fields with me when checking the sheep; but as soon as a youngster shows the first signs of chasing them I only exercise him well away from the flock to prevent him developing bad habits. Then, if I do find myself anywhere near sheep when out walking with him, I keep him on a lead until the sheep are out of sight again.

EARLY INTEREST IN SHEEP

While I like to see a puppy of between four and six months showing an interest in the sheep by chasing them, because that means I will have something to work on later, I only allow this to happen once. If I show him the sheep and he is not interested, I keep him away from them for another month or so and then try again; eventually he will take off after them. Then I keep him away from all casual contact with sheep and wait until he is ten to twelve months of age before thinking about formal training. Whilst an experienced handler might be able to start a little earlier because he knows what he is doing, a novice should never think of doing so. Some people think that, if a youngster is pulling on the lead when walked through sheep, or tries to dash in amongst them, he is ready for training because he is keen. They fail to take into account that below the age of around twelve months he may not be mentally ready, nor sufficiently mature to develop his powers of concentration. Beginning formal training, however short those first lessons are, is a big change for a youngster – he needs to be mature enough to accept the learning and work. Rushing things is always a mistake when training any animal.

A young pup should never be allowed to go to sheep on his own — if he does, he is likely to chase them and/or hold them up to a corner for long periods — both bad habits which must not be allowed to develop. People have brought their young dogs to me for training saying, 'Oh yes, he's ready to train — if he gets loose, he goes straight into a field and he'll hold the sheep in a corner all day.' This does not indicate to me that the dog is ready for training, but it does tell me a lot about the owner — and that the early training of that dog is going to be more difficult than it should be!

Problems can also be caused if a young dog has been held on a lead by the side of the handler 'for a bit of experience' when fetching sheep into the yards. Experience it is, but of the wrong variety; if he gets used to being on the same side of the sheep as the handler all the time, it will be difficult to teach him to go to the front of the handler and to the far side of the sheep.

SIX MONTHS OLD

By the time he is six months old a puppy should be bold, self-assured and inquisitive, know his name, be happy to return to his handler when called, be able to travel happily in a vehicle, be used to wearing a collar at least some of the time, be more or less house-trained and, most importantly, he should have had a happy puppyhood. The pup should also be beginning to lie down when the command 'Lie down' is given. (When working, sheepdogs should never sit as well-trained members of other breeds are trained to do. They can be moving, or standing on their feet, or lying down — but never sitting.) A puppy of this age should also have grown to like his owner so much that his main aim in life is to spend time with him. There should be a developing desire to please linked with moments of defiance, indicating that the puppy has some spirit and a mind of his own. This is the time when I can begin to widen the pup's experience even more in preparation for formal training.

BASIC TRAINING BEGINS

It is essential for any dog of mine to stop when asked and to come to me when called, particularly when working with sheep; this is the area on which I can work between the ages of six and twelve months. So by the time he is introduced to his small training flock my youngster knows that 'Down' and 'That'll do' mean he should lie down and come to me, respectively, and also recognizes the whistle command for the 'Down'. After around six months' work, first on a verbal command of 'Down' only, then later using voice and whistle, I can be sure that the pup will go down every time he is told to do so, and come to me when called; he will therefore have this knowledge when taken out to sheep for the first time. On the first few times out, however, the pup will be far too excited to stop — but the important thing is to ensure he knows what is required of him by then. As he settles with his sheep, he will eventually begin to go down when told. If I can stop my dog when he is on sheep, then I can give him, and myself, the chance to cool things off and settle down before starting again.

TEACHING 'DOWN' AND 'THAT'LL DO'

To teach a pup to go down, I first loop a length of string through his collar to help me to keep control and prevent the pup from running off. Then I kneel down in front of him, stroking him and speaking quietly to reassure him. I hold the string near to the collar, say 'Down', and at the same time pull down on the string with one hand while firmly pushing the dog's back down with the other. I keep the dog down for about half a minute, stroking him all the time and repeating the 'Down' command. Then I let him get to his feet, praising and patting him before repeating the procedure. After that, the lesson is over. I use the words 'That'll do' to tell the dog to come to me and to signify that work is over, and by using these words from the start the youngster soon learns to differentiate between work and play periods.

As the 'Down' training continues, I gradually increase the length of time the dog is lying down. Once he will stay down reliably, while he is in that position I slowly increase my distance from him. I do this by taking first one step back from him before returning to the dog and saying, 'That'll do.' Gradually I move further from him, continually repeating the 'Down' command, before either retracing my steps or calling him to me. With the more biddable youngsters I can usually dispense with the string quite quickly, but the more pushy dog might persist longer in getting to his feet and moving from his down position. If he does this, I just growl quietly, put him back where he was, slip the string through his collar to maintain control, repeat the command and back away again, holding the string loosely. Eventually, after repetition of this kind, the dog becomes more reliable and I can dispense with the string.

From moving backwards from the dog, I then begin to generalize my position by moving myself around a little more, with the dog still lying down, and then saying, 'That'll do' to signify that he can move from that position. Then I will pat my knee to get the dog to come to me, using his name and making a great fuss of him when he does so.

THE NOVICE TRAINER

Before I explain how I start training youngsters with sheep, I want to offer a word of advice to those who have never done this before. I would recommend any novice trainer with his first sheepdog to enrol in an ATB class, or to get private lessons from an established handler, before he ever takes his dog out to sheep for training. He will then be able to run the first lessons in a controlled environment with suitable sheep and an experienced trainer to demonstrate, advise and correct when things are going wrong. The owner is going to be more relaxed because he is not trying to battle on alone, the lessons will go better, and both handler and dog will be able to build up some good experience together. Remember that I enrolled in ATB classes and solicited help from many experienced handlers before I became a competent trainer, and living with a superb sheepdog trainer like Jim was an enormous help.

One warning — never make the mistake of allowing your youngster to run with his mother or an older dog as a way of training. It is the worst thing you can do because the pup will learn to chase the older dog in play as it works the sheep, and that is the last thing you want him to do. I always remember the farmer who brought his six-year-old bitch to me with her three-year-old daughter. Because he had been too busy to train the daughter when she was a youngster he always took her out to sheep with her mother, never on her own. By the time he decided to do something about getting her properly trained, it was too late. When I saw the daughter, who showed signs of good innate herding ability, she was refusing to work without her mother and had no interest in sheep if taken out to them on her own. Irreparable damage had been done, and I wondered what the farmer would do when the older bitch died and he was left with a useless working dog.

REWARDS AND SANCTIONS

Many novices ask me what rewards I give my dogs in training when they have done well. They are probably thinking in terms of bits of meat or chocolate drops, but I usually find that an approving tone of voice and affectionate patting are all that is needed to tell a dog he has done well.

I am also asked about sanctions. In the early stages these are not necessary if training is being done correctly, because the dog is never allowed to do anything really wrong. Later on in training, when sanctions might be needed, growling and a displeased tone of voice are usually sufficient. The greatest sanction I ever apply is with an older dog who is defying me for some reason. Then I will pick him up by his ruff, growl loudly, look straight into his eyes and give him a good shake before putting him down and returning to the lesson. I have never hit a dog in my life and never intend to − it is a totally unnecessary and demeaning act for both trainer and dog, and always counter-productive in the long term.

SERIOUS TRAINING BEGINS

I am fortunate in having a small stone-walled field of a couple of acres which is ideal for starting youngsters off on sheep. I also use a trained dog − currently Trim − to help me keep the sheep from breaking away, because it is absolutely crucial that those first few lessons with sheep are well controlled and go as they should. If the pup has a bad experience − if he is butted by a ewe, or is allowed to chase them all over the place or to grip or hold the sheep up against a wall − this type of behaviour can stay with him for the rest of his life. So it is important to get things right from the very first day.

Sheepdog at work

Young dogs show various reactions when I first take them out to begin their training on sheep, but I already have a fair idea of what each individual is going to be like because I have been observing his responses to other situations up to this time. A youngster might be keen, shy, show too much 'eye' or lack concentration – or he might not want to work at all. Whichever type of dog I find myself with, right from the beginning I must instil into him the idea that he needs to hold the sheep to me, and all the movements I make at this point will be to achieve this aim. The trained dog I take out at the same time will gather the sheep and keep them in the right place throughout the lesson – a well-trained dog is essential for this task because it will take notice of my commands without diverting the youngster's attention from the sheep, and will lie quietly out of the way when not needed.

TYPE OF SHEEP

When the day arrives for me to take the pup out for his first lesson on sheep, I will get eight to ten ewe lambs — hoggs, as sheep people call them — together in my small, walled field. I use hoggs because they are more amenable than crafty old ewes, while rams (or tups) should never be used for training because they can get too aggressive. From now on until he can be trusted to stay at my side when not working sheep, the pup is taken out on a piece of string looped through his collar. I do not tie it, because I am going to need to let it slide through when I let the pup go.

WALKING OUT TO THE SHEEP

I approach the sheep from an angle, depending on which side I am intending the dog to run out from. As I go out, I have the dog on the side away from the sheep. He is facing the way he is to go, we are both looking and moving in that direction, and my head and body are inclined forwards — this is all part of the body language which I will use throughout training to reinforce my intentions, and which will still be used when I am handling my fully trained dog. When I go out to the post at the beginning of a trial, I approach it from the left, dog on my right, if I am going to send him on a right-hand outrun to lift the sheep; and from the right, with the dog on my left, if I intend a left-hand outrun. Thus, without a word being spoken, the dog is already aware of what is expected of him.

THE PUP SETS OFF

In the training field with my pup, I send the experienced Trim out to bring the sheep into the centre of the field as the young dog and I move forwards — the youngster on my right side this first time, with Trim at the back of the sheep, holding them to me. Turning to my right, and with the pup slightly to the back of me, but facing to his right, I tell him to lie down. As soon as he does this, I slip the string off by allowing it to slide through his collar. Then I make a 'shhh' sound to encourage him to set off. As the dog begins to run forward, I walk slightly to the right of the sheep and towards them to make sure there is no gap. I can then, if necessary, stop the dog from coming in

Lie down.

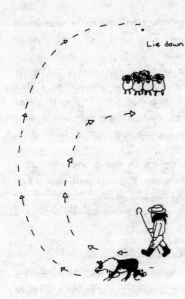

The dog in the correct position behind the sheep at 12 o'clock from me.

Setting the dog off to the Left.

(similarly to the right)

I stand between the dog and the sheep to make sure that he sets off properly.

131

front of the sheep if he tries to change direction, and he is more likely to go to the far side of them as I move. This is all done very close to hand, within a radius of 12 to 15 feet.

Once the pup reaches the far side of the sheep, and is at twelve o'clock to me, I stop him. Then, as soon as he goes down, I start to move backwards, varying my movements just a yard or so to either side, or pushing the weight of the sheep towards the pup before moving myself backwards again, thus encouraging the dog to keep moving on the far side of them.

If a youngster shows a distinct preference for going one way rather than the other, this must be nipped in the bud. He will need extra encouragement to go to the side he does not like so much but, providing this is given, he will soon get used to running round equally well, and willingly, both ways.

DIFFERENT REACTIONS

A confident youngster will usually get the hang of running to the twelve o'clock position quite quickly, following the sheep and holding them to me; but with a shyer, less confident dog I need to keep talking to him all the time to give reassurance and to encourage him to come forward. Initially, this kind of pup is often less ready to move to the far side of the sheep, which means I might have to move round the sheep myself to encourage him into the twelve o'clock position. If, when the youngster is at this position, he is reluctant to come forward, I use Trim to begin to move the sheep quietly towards me. This will encourage the pup to follow them. When he is moving, I tell Trim to 'Lie down, stay there' until she is needed again. Once this type of youngster grasps the idea of getting to the far side of the sheep, I will often let him move with them without stopping him first, as I do not want to inhibit his actions.

If I have a keen young dog – one who moves off as soon as I pull the string out – he will usually run round to the far side of the sheep straightaway; but it will be more difficult to stop him and keep him in the correct place at the back of the sheep. I have to encourage this kind of youngster to keep to the back whenever he tries to come round to the front of them, so I block his path and turn him back to twelve o'clock as he begins to run round the sheep.

I must admit that I like training the keen youngsters better because

I know from the start that I will finish with a good workdog, if not a trials dog. With the others, it takes a bit longer before I have this certainty.

EYE

I do not like to see too much 'eye' in young dogs, although a little is needed to help them to maintain concentration. If they have a lot of 'eye' they will tend to stalk the sheep, or be reluctant to move, remaining stationary and staring at them, or refusing to get off their tummies. It is essential that I break the dog's concentration, make him listen to me and keep him on the go: I do this by pushing the sheep towards the dog more, so that he has to move off his tummy to take the weight of them — this means either moving round the sheep, quietly keeping them in a close bunch, or starting to move towards the sheep, usually as a preliminary to moving or turning them. With this kind of dog I have to ensure that things are in continual motion and never static. So the sheep must always be very free-moving, even if this means changing my training sheep frequently. There is no doubt that such dogs can be very hard work, but if the trainer can keep the youngster and sheep moving around continuously in these early stages of training, the dog will not develop the habit of being mesmerized by his sheep.

THE END OF THE LESSON

As soon as I have got the dog holding the sheep to me and moving to right or left to keep them to me, then I tell him to 'Lie down', repeating the command all the time as I walk towards him and, if necessary, walking through the sheep to reach him. I never call a young dog to me when the lesson is at an end, because he is too young and inexperienced to come off the sheep and all the way to me without going wrong. As soon as I reach the dog I slip the string through his collar and praise him; then I say 'That'll do' and together we walk away from the sheep and off the field. The dog has to be under control to prevent him from running back to his sheep, as he will invariably want to do because I am finishing the lesson while he is still interested in them.

I always stop the lesson when the pup is still keen and eager to run —

133

two to five minutes on the sheep is plenty at this stage. Many novice handlers make the mistake of going on for too long so that the dog gets bored — if there are signs of sniffing, yawning, eating sheep droppings or his eye being caught by something else, then more harm than good has been done. He should be taken back to his kennel a happy, interested dog, not a bored one.

THE PUP WHO GRIPS

If, when I take him out to sheep for the first few times, I find I have a hard type of youngster who keeps coming in to grip them, then I need to maintain more control over what he is doing. But I never make the mistake of shouting and hollering at him. I will talk to this dog more than usual, and work close to hand for considerably longer in the training programme than with the dog who does not go in to grip. The secret with a 'gripper' is to stop him going in to nip the sheep before he actually does it. All the time I will be looking for overt signs of evil intent: slight flattening of the dog's ears, intent facial expression and tensing of his body. Once recognized, they give the game away; when this happens, I immediately increase my verbal contact with the dog. Talking continuously to him and controlling him with the tone

I walk through the sheep to stop the dog from coming in and I make him run out again.

of my voice, which will become more firm and commanding, I walk through the sheep to stop the dog from coming in and to make him cast out — run round the flock to end up behind them — again.

If he is a persistent gripper, I will actually stop the dog; but if possible I prefer to keep him moving freely on the far side of the sheep. Persistent gripping is usually a sign that the young dog is lacking in confidence, so I need not only to persuade him that gripping is wrong, but also to give plenty of reassurance and lots of praise when he eventually gets things right. It can add weeks to this stage of training, but patience and perseverance are everything and, given sufficient time working close to hand, the youngster will eventually keep moving behind his sheep without feeling the need to go in and grip to show that he is the boss.

DEVELOPMENT OF BALANCE AND THE LIFT

I work close to the sheep in these early stages because I have to make the dogs understand that they must hold the sheep to me and not to a fence or a wall. I am trying to nurture the dog's natural 'balance' and 'feel' for sheep — his ability to maintain the correct distance between himself and the sheep in order to control them — which will provide the basis for all other aspects of his training. Not only does the dog need to balance the sheep to me — I need to balance the sheep to him. So it is important to take time, get it right and not force the pace.

The dog's 'feel' for sheep gradually develops over a period of time as he learns how to gauge the optimum distance from which to maintain contact but not to unsettle them. If he is a bit tight at first I never worry about it — I know that, if I am patient and don't rush the dog, he will eventually learn to leave enough space. Some dogs can control sheep from a greater distance than others, and they all need to learn that different types of sheep, with their varying reactions to dogs, need different working distances for that control to be maintained. In the early days, working close to hand all the time, I am laying the foundations for the dog to develop his own natural ability to do this — I am encouraging and not forcing him, and that is one of the reasons it takes so long to achieve. Lad, with his great natural 'feel' for sheep, taught me that all types of sheep need a different approach from the dog in lifting and working them. Lad has always instinctively known which method to adopt as soon as he sets eyes on the sheep; some dogs take longer than others to acquire this skill, but they will get there in the end with good training.

Very occasionally, a really hard young dog will persist in getting too close to the sheep when he runs to the twelve o'clock position. When this happens I growl at him, stop him, walk towards him through the sheep (still growling) and tell him to get back. This is another area where Jim's teaching was invaluable. Before meeting him, I had never seen anybody who was prepared to take so much time to let a young dog learn how to balance sheep quite naturally, without a harsh word being spoken to make him stay further away from the sheep or to come closer to them. I discovered that the dog would develop this natural balance if I was moving the sheep around in the right way and keeping myself in the right position — at six o'clock to the dog's twelve o'clock position. I also learned the hard way that it is very easy, when concentrating on all this, to get oneself backed up against a wall, so now I try to keep track of my bearings at all times as dog, sheep and I move around the field.

Once the youngster is running round to the back of the sheep to his left or right, will stop when commanded, has learnt his correct distance from the sheep, and moves quietly to balance them, he is on his way to learning to 'lift' the sheep correctly, without upsetting them, and to move forwards with them towards the handler (the beginning of the 'fetch').

GETTING SHEEP FROM A WALL OR CORNER

By the time the young dog has been to the sheep five or six times, he will be beginning to move freely to balance them as I move forwards, backwards and sideways around the middle of the field. He then needs to start learning how to bring sheep away from a wall or corner and, providing I have taught my youngster to hold the sheep to me, there should be no problems.

I gradually allow myself and the sheep to move nearer and nearer to a wall or hedge, just getting a few yards closer with each day's lesson. Keeping the sheep between me and the dog, I continue to move in all directions, sometimes with my back towards the wall, sometimes with the wall on my side, sometimes with the wall in front of me, but still some distance away. During the next few days, whenever the dog is in the large gap between sheep and wall I tell him to lie down, then to bring the sheep to me as I walk backwards, away from the wall and towards the middle of the field. Eventually we will be working only a few yards away from the gap between sheep and wall, and the dog will have grown used to it. By working in this way, it will not be many days before the youngster is going quite confidently and naturally along the wall side to get to the back of his sheep.

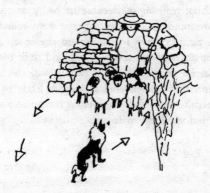

Encouraging the young dog to move
sheep out of a corner as he changes
places with me.

Occasionally a dog will realize that something is different, see the wall and decide he is not keen on running between it and the sheep. So I need to give him extra help in order to boost his confidence. With the sheep close to the wall, I move to stand near the dog and then 'shhh' him round, speaking words of encouragement and reassurance all the time. If this fails to work, I immediately widen the gap to enable him to get between the sheep and wall easily, then narrow the gap once more and try again. Once a dog has the confidence to go between a wall and his sheep he will get great enjoyment out of doing so. After that, getting sheep out of a corner is just a continuation of this manoeuvre.

I remember being in tears once when I first went to Jim's, because I could not get my dog to move sheep from a corner. It was Jim who taught me how to remedy this problem (after ticking me off for allowing it to happen in the first place). He told me to put myself in the corner with the sheep, and the dog on the far side of them; then, gradually pushing the sheep towards the dog, getting him to hold them to me, talking quietly all the time to maintain contact and give the dog confidence, I backed gradually along the wall and out of the corner. The dog moved to balance the sheep, going gradually into the corner himself as I moved out towards the field. As he changed places with me, he moved into the corner without realizing it. Because he had grown used to holding the sheep at the point of balance, the dog went round them to keep himself in the right position in relation to the sheep and me, and it encouraged him to hold the sheep to me and walk out of the corner with them. Careful training to work near a wall, as described above, usually pre-empts this problem; but it is quite likely to happen to the novice who needs to learn that the remedy is relatively simple — as Jim taught me in that short, sharp lesson.

10
EXTENDING THE TRAINING

LENGTHENING THE RUN TO THE BACK OF THE SHEEP

When I am satisfied that the dog is ready to go a step further in his training, I can very gradually begin to increase the distance the dog needs to run to get to the back of the sheep. The first time I do this, I stand just a couple of paces further back from the sheep than before, shushing the dog out to the left or right. Then, providing he reaches the back of the sheep from this point, I increase the distance from them by a couple more paces each time he is sent out, always watching the dog carefully in case he shows any signs of loss of confidence — such as hesitation, looking back at me, or running to the sheep at an angle before getting round to the back. If any of these things happen I stop the dog, walk through the sheep to him, then send him out from that position, close to the sheep again (something he is used to doing and will therefore enjoy), before taking him back to his kennel.

The next time I take the dog out, and for the next few lessons, I backtrack and set him off from near to the sheep again until he is relaxed and confident once more. Then I begin to lengthen the distance again until the dog is able to run out for up to 30 yards — in other words he is beginning to develop a short outrun, which is a step forward from simply running a few yards to get to the back of the sheep. I never allow the distance to increase to more than that at this point because I still need to be close enough to the dog to maintain adequate control over his movements. The length of time it takes to reach this stage will vary from dog to dog, but it will take many weeks to ensure that he achieves it every time — and that he runs out equally well from whichever side he is sent out. The longer outruns come later when the dog has acquired greater confidence and reliability, and is able to flank properly close to hand — that is, when he is able to move correctly to right or left when working close to the handler.

LEARNING MORE VERBAL COMMANDS

As I start to lengthen the outrun to the back of the sheep I begin to use the verbal commands for left and right. Let's say I shush the dog out to the right. Once he has begun to run in that direction I say quietly 'Away here' (my command for the dog to go to his right). If I am sending him off from the left, I give him the left-hand command, 'Come bye', once he has begun to run in that direction. It is also a good idea to use a slightly different tone of voice for each of these commands — I say 'Come bye' in a low voice, and 'Away here' in a slightly higher tone. These traditional commands for left and right have some variations up and down the country, but any word or words the handler prefers may be used as long as they are noticeably different in sound from each other and are reasonably short. The use of two words rather than one can, however, be an advantage at a later stage in training. If you want a dog to take his time you use both words in a drawn out way; but if you want the dog to get a move on, you use just the first word sharply and tersely. By this time, the dog will be walking away from the sheep without any restraint other than the sound of my voice, and can be relied upon not to run back to the sheep.

INCREASING THE DOG'S EXPERIENCE

Once the dog will run out reliably to either side to a distance of up to 30 yards, I begin to introduce other small areas of experience to provide variety and to get him used to being in different places with sheep. My present youngster, Molly, is now at this stage and I take her with me when I am going out to rudd the tups — to mark their chests with paint, which will rub off on the ewes they have served and so identify them — or to gather the ewes. Molly lies down at my feet while I send a trained dog out to gather the sheep and bring them towards me. Once they are no more than 30 yards away, I tell the trained dog to lie down. Then I send Molly out to run to the far side of the flock and bring them to me, before holding them to me as I deal with the tups. This gives my young dog a chance to work with more sheep and in different fields.

In the ATB classes which I run, I find that few novice handlers walk about enough when out on the field with sheep and a young dog; they also tend not to keep up adequate contact with the youngster, which is achieved by talking quietly to him all the time while moving around the field. This continual contact is essential to build the dog's confidence and to reinforce what is being said to him; so my first task is to encourage the new handlers to develop enough confidence in themselves to talk to their dogs continually and to use the field to full advantage.

FLANKING

Once the dog will run out to either side of the sheep, hold them to me, move to balance the sheep as I move myself around, and walk after the sheep when I am walking backwards away from him, and once the dog is making a proper-length outrun to his sheep each time, then I can move on to the next stage. Now I work on making sure that the dog's flanking movements are made squarely off the sheep — turning his body at right-angles to the sheep when he changes direction, and not running gradually closer to them.

I have already been doing some work on this by moving the weight of the sheep towards the dog to make sure he has to flank squarely to take that weight. As time goes on and the distances between me, the sheep and the dog lengthen, it is important to keep these flanking movements square, and to ensure that the dog does not begin to move towards his sheep when he is commanded to go to left or right. When I set the dog off from my side to run to the back of the sheep, he is already at right-angles to them because he is at my side, facing the way he is to go, and I am between him and the sheep — the beginning of a square movement off the sheep.

Square flanking — correct and incorrect.

If I have a pushy, eager dog, running to the correct side but slightly towards his sheep as he flanks, I have to do something to correct him. I get the dog to make short movements. I tell him to lie down; then I walk through the sheep and, when I reach the dog's side, send him off again to go round them. I allow him to go a short distance, stop him, walk to him again, stand between him and the sheep and send him off once more, making sure that he has to make a square movement round me to run out to the sheep. Good early work can obviate a lot of extra training and enable many dogs to flank squarely, but others will only do so when I have insisted on those short, square movements to get the message across. The dog must learn to take a flanking command to left or right from wherever he is in relation to the sheep and me, and he must turn his whole body to face the direction in which he is going. It is also important that he does not develop the habit of flanking off too widely and sending himself into orbit, losing contact with his sheep — this should not happen if I am working on these movements close to hand all the time until he has got it right. The dog is learning to flank quietly as well as squarely, to maintain his own working distance from the sheep and to have contact with them without getting too close and upsetting them.

Again, as at every stage of training, all dogs vary and will progress at different rates. Trim is very quiet and gentle with sheep and does not need exaggerated flanking movements, but Royale Moss was a different type altogether. He was a pushy, keen youngster, so I had to insist on him flanking squarely at all times during his training, which I had to reinforce throughout the four years I had him.

DRIVING

When beginning to teach a dog to drive sheep you have to ask him to come off balance, and he will be learning to walk behind his sheep in a position other than the twelve o'clock one to which he has become accustomed. I never ask a dog to do this before he knows his verbal commands thoroughly, is flanking squarely and will stop every time he is asked.

When the dog brings the sheep across the field towards me, I let them begin to drift past me to one side and encourage the dog to follow them — I stay close to the dog at this point to give him confidence. As he draws level with me I turn to face the direction in which he is moving, walking alongside the dog as he continues behind his sheep, telling him to 'walk on' and encouraging him all the time to let him know that he is doing the right thing. Then I flank the dog to send him to the far side of the sheep once more and bring them back to me. I allow the sheep to drift past me again (on the other side this time) with the dog following them while I turn to be at his side, giving encouragement.

Without knowing it, the dog is beginning to drive his sheep past me — whereas before he has always just held them to me or brought them down the field to me. The first few times we do this, I only try it once or twice during the course of the lesson to ensure the dog spends most of the time working at well-known movements.

When the sheep first begin to drift past me, the dog might try to move himself round to the point of balance to hold the sheep to me again. If so, I never make an issue of it but allow him to carry on, working the sheep around the field a bit longer, and then we try again. As always, I talk to the dog continuously and never allow the situation to develop into a contest between us.

Beginning to drive. The sheep are allowed to drift past me and I encourage the dog to follow the sheep.

As the youngster gets used to driving the sheep past me I tend to drop further and further behind him, but I am still walking continually forwards to ensure that the dog is never more than about 20 feet from me. If he shows signs of looking back at me I immediately tell him to 'Walk on' and move closer to him to provide reassurance, perhaps walking alongside him again for a couple of days before allowing the distances gradually to lengthen once more.

It can take several weeks to get the dog confident enough to drive away the sheep for a good distance on his own, and I never go on for long with this part of the lesson. I constantly alternate it with other moves to make sure the dog gets neither bored nor confused. In fact I never concentrate on one single manoueuvre in any lesson — otherwise the dog would lose his concentration. So, as teaching time lengthens, I need to vary the content as much as possible.

By this time, the youngster has progressed sufficiently to be taken out to larger numbers of sheep, in the fields or on the fells, to go walkabout for miles up hills, across streams and through gateways. This is when the driving training, begun in the small field, becomes well reinforced, with me still walking no more than 20 yards behind the dog to give him confidence as we cover the miles together. This enables the dog to begin to adapt his training into the working situation in a natural way.

Don't worry about him! He's failed his driving test.

FLANKING FROM THE DRIVING POSITION

Once the dog seems quite happy driving, the next step is to teach him to flank off the sheep as he drives them away from me — something entirely new to him. I walk slightly behind the dog and to his left, and give the command for him to flank to the left. Then, as soon as he has moved a couple of yards in that direction, I stop him and tell him to 'Walk on' to continue driving. Next I repeat this to the other side.

Now the dog can move on to another stage in his flanking training Up to this time, other than running out from my side, he has always had the sheep between himself and me; but I am asking him to flank between me and the sheep. When he is able to do the short flanking movements just in front of me, as described above, I move a little further back. Then I call the dog to me with 'That'll do' and pat my knee in encouragement. When the dog gets closer, I get him to to keep running in front of me and round to the other side of the sheep by giving him the flanking command for that side. Some dogs will want to run behind me, but I can stop them doing this by standing with my back to a wall the first few times, so that they have to run between me and the sheep to get round.

It took me a long time to teach Max to drive: he needed continual encouragement, with me walking at his side to increase his confidence. But Trim was remarkably easy — she was a natural driver and from the beginning would quite happily take the sheep all the way up the field away from me, plodding along behind them until they were almost out of sight.

CROSS-DRIVING

This is simply driving the sheep at a different angle across the field. It should follow naturally from the driving procedure by varying the position of the dog on the clock.

SHEDDING

The ability to shed a single sheep or a group from the rest of the flock is another essential part of training. If a young dog always comes straight to the handler whenever he is asked, shedding should present no problems — it is merely an extension of this simple procedure.

I begin to introduce shedding at the same time as I am teaching driving — again, carefully and gradually. I have twenty to thirty hoggs between me and the dog, close to hand. I tell the dog to lie down on the far side of the sheep. Then I move forwards through them to split them and make a good gap. I incline my body in the direction of the packet of sheep I will eventually want the dog to take off, move partly through the space towards the dog, put my hand in the gap, and

Shedding . A gap is made.
The dog is called through and
assisted in taking the shed sheep away.

then say 'That'll do. This,' as I pat my knee for the dog to come to me.

As the sheep begin to split he will probably want to go round the whole lot in an effort to keep them together. But I give him plenty of encouragement to ensure that he comes through the gap towards me. When he reaches me, I praise the dog and tell him to lie him down between the two lots of sheep. By this time I have my eyes half on the dog and half on the sheep that are to be taken off. Then I turn towards the chosen packet of sheep for them to be taken away, encouraging the dog to drive them while walking at my side. So now he is once again in a position he knows – the one for driving. Then I send him round this packet of sheep, getting him to hold them to me and moving around, leaving the other sheep behind me.

I encourage the dog to enjoy working with this first lot of sheep and to forget about the other group, because he is learning to concentrate on the packet of sheep chosen by the handler. I do not allow him to go to those behind me until I want him to do so. When I am ready, I allow the two lots of sheep to drift back together again.

When first teaching the shed, I say, 'That'll do. This'. The 'That'll do' is already familiar to the dog and means he must ignore the sheep and come to me. 'This' is the command for shedding. As time goes on, and the dog begins to understand the meaning of 'This', I am able to dispense with the 'That'll do' and just use 'This' for a speedy shed. I talk quietly to the dog while preparing to shed – reinforcing the 'Lie down' while he is waiting. Then I put a lot of emphasis on the 'This' command when I want him to come through the sheep.

Is *that* the shed?

For several weeks I only practise the shed once or twice during a lesson, at first making a wide gap. Eventually I can narrow it to the stage where my dog will come through the sheep like a rocket with barely a gap at all. It is not long before the dog knows by my movements that I am preparing to shed sheep and that he will need to come through the slightest gap to reach me and take a packet away. Most dogs love this manoeuvre if it is properly done and they are encouraged to enjoy what they are doing; once fully trained, they are a joy to watch.

THE SINGLE

Once a dog will shed well every time and can turn on to the sheep I want him to take away, I begin to reduce the size of the packet to be taken off. Eventually we will get down to splitting just one sheep off and taking it away, which is known as the single.

THE LOOK BACK

The 'Look back' or 'Turn back' — meaning to go back for more sheep — can develop quite naturally from the shedding procedure in a smaller field; six to seven acres is ideal. Once the dog is getting quite good at shedding, is driving well and I am beginning to put whistle commands to fuller use, then we can try the 'Look back'.

The first thing I do is to shed some sheep off, turn the dog on to them and drive them away from the others, with me walking at the side of the dog. I then encourage the dog to hold the sheep to me as I gradually move until I am facing both packets of sheep with the dog facing me, his back to the second group of sheep. Making sure that this group is still well in sight and not too far away, I then flank the dog to the side of the first lot of sheep. I tell the dog to 'Lie down, look back.' He will not understand what 'Look back' means, but will realize it is something different and will tend to look around him. As soon as I notice that the dog has spotted the second lot of sheep I repeat 'Look back', immediately followed by the appropriate flanking command for him to run round the second lot of sheep to lift them and bring them back to join the others.

Every now and again at this stage, I practise the 'Look back' from either side of the first packet of sheep. I do it close to hand and then, as the dog gets more confident, I move myself gradually further away from him before telling him to look back. Then I increase the distance between the two packets of sheep, using different parts of the field, always remembering the importance of having the lie down, look back and flanking sequence of commands to maintain proper control. Eventually, the time arrives when I can send my dog on the 'Look back' to collect a packet of sheep which may be out of sight. There is a great sense of achievement when that stage is reached.

PENNING SHEEP

I do not teach my dogs to drive sheep into a pen as such, and never have a pen in the training field. I practise for penning by getting the

Lie down.

The 'turn back'

dog to make fine, short, square flanking movements with the sheep up against a wall. I get him to work very close to the sheep without upsetting them and to move quietly — gradually learning to go only one step at a time, or to alter the position of his body slightly one way or another to control a small movement of the sheep. If he is capable of these refined movements when working close to the sheep by a wall, the dog has all the ability he needs to get sheep into the pen at a trial or in the work situation.

CONCLUDING THOUGHTS ON TRAINING

There is no doubt in my mind that training a Border Collie for work and sheepdog trials is an art. The trainer must be capable of continually learning and adapting to provide the required knowledge and flexibility of approach; a sound understanding of the psychology underlying the reasons for canine behaviour is also needed. I think my greatest pleasure in life now comes from undertaking the training of a young dog, watching his progress, sorting out any problems which might arise and, above all, developing an ever-increasing bond and partnership with that dog.

In the early stages, the short training sessions should be like a game which the puppy can enjoy — all training is a serious matter, but a young dog does not realize this if he is enjoying what is going on. Later he will go out to training sessions, work or sheepdog trialling in the same happy frame of mind. A dog should never be forced to do anything; instead, his natural instincts should be encouraged to develop in a controlled, intelligent and enjoyable way which enables him to use his brain while being prepared to accept commands when given.

If I ever find that things are getting out of hand at any stage in the training (this happens less often as I gain in experience), or the dog is getting confused and failing to respond to what I am trying to teach him, I count up to five, catch him, put him on a lead and take him back to his kennel. Then I give him a few days' rest before taking him out to the sheep again. I can guarantee that he will return to work with renewed vigour, enthusiasm and enjoyment. The same thing applies when a dog seems to have lost some of his freshness and sparkle (or I have!), either on the training field or at work.

Even with a fully trained dog, it is sometimes necessary to work him close to hand from time to time to refine his movements and tighten up his reactions to commands, rather in the way one needs to keep schooling a horse to keep it at its optimum level. The dogs usually enjoy these postgraduate training sessions, which hone their skills and continue to reinforce the partnership to the benefit of handler, dog and sheep, at work or at trials.

All training consists of an element of going forward, returning to an earlier stage, resting self and dog from time to time, teasing out reasons for things going wrong, and adjusting one's methods in the light of experience. I learn something new from every dog I train, which helps make it all so interesting and challenging to me. It also makes the business of sheepdog training seem complicated and nerve-racking to the beginner. But, providing you keep learning and adjusting, give the dog a good start, read books on training, watch some of the training videos now on the market and, above all, watch the experts on the trials field and pick their brains, you will get there in the end — and sooner than you think. Training a sheepdog is unlike any other dog training because the handler is trying to develop the dog's instincts and ability to work — less a matter of dominating than of enabling and developing. It is far more than a matter of teaching a dog to stop, start, go left, go right and so on.

Trainers must remember that every dog is an individual and needs to be treated as such. As the dog progresses and learns to work for and with the handler, the bond between them grows so strong that the dog becomes an extension of the person who has trained him. This is why, when a trained dog goes to a new owner, the onus is on that person to take the time to get to know the dog really well, and vice versa. Depending on the type of dog and handler, this can take months to achieve, but it is the basis of all their future work together. The partnership between a handler and his dog is a sensitive thing, and the weight of responsibility for a successful outcome, at work and play, rests firmly on the handler every time.

11
TELEVISION APPEARANCES

Shortly before lambing started in 1989, a television crew arrived at Richard's farm to film me at work with my dogs for the children's programme *Blue Peter*. That was when I discovered that I enjoyed performing in front of the cameras. The presenter of the programme, Mark Curry, was also there to interview me, and he followed me round all day as I did my work. At one point I loaded some sugar beet nuts and sheep nuts in the back of the Land Rover and we set off to feed the sheep; that was when Mark nearly came to a sticky end.

The ewes need a lot of extra feed before lambing, and I knew from past experience that they will move at considerable speed, knocking over anything in their path, to get at favourite food such as sheep nuts. To protect myself from their onslaught during winter feeding I always have a dog at my side, and as I scatter the nuts I begin at the top of an incline where the land is dry and then go back in the opposite direction to give me further protection. Of course, Mark knew nothing of these strategies when I sent Trim off to gather sheep from a high pasture. By the time she began to bring the flock down towards us I had slit open one of the bags with my knife, handed the bag to Mark and asked him to scatter the nuts in a line well away from the Land Rover. Off went Mark, the sheep in hot pursuit, no dog to protect him and no idea what to expect.

By the time they reached Mark the ewes were travelling at a fair old lick, despite their increased weight and girth. Within seconds he was swept off his feet and disappeared into a throng of woolly backs. It took Mark quite a time to get to his feet again, partly because he was laughing so much and partly because each time he tried to get up he was knocked over again by the sheep. I was hysterical with laughter and so were the cameramen, who had managed to record the incident on film. The BBC has since used this sequence in several programmes devoted to the times when things go wrong during filming!

Two years later, when I was going to appear on *Blue Peter* again, I was in a bit of a panic because I had no vehicle and therefore no way of getting my dogs, ducks and props down to London. It was the time of the local Muker agricultural show, and it was there that I met a solicitor named Richard Hammersley. When Richard learned of my predicament he offered to lend me his Range Rover, and ever since he has always been Richard Range Rover to me. Accompanied by Anne (J) and Trim, Richard drove me down south, towing my trailer with its cargo of props and ducks all the way to his home in Henley-on-Thames where he kept the Range Rover.

The presenter on that second *Blue Peter* programme was Yvette Fielding, a lady with a well-developed sense of humour who wanted me to demonstrate how versatile a sheepdog needs to be in its work. The filming took place in the *Blue Peter* garden at the back of the BBC studio and, as there was already a pond there, we decided to use that for the finale. Everything went well until the ducks slid down into the water, and emerged with their lower halves and feet covered in thick black mud. It bothered the ducks not at all, but the camera crew, Yvette and I subsided into the BBC canteen for a much-needed cup of coffee. While we were there, the ducks waddled across to the open door and into the kitchens which opened on to the garden — and were rewarded by the cook, who fed them with pieces of bread until our return.

There was an amusing sequel to the making of these films. I video-ed them when they were shown on television and now, whenever I watch them, Trim, who is a real telly addict, trots round to the back of the set to find me and the sheep. In the part where I was filmed giving the Fawcett children their tea she goes behind the TV again to look for them, then back once more to find the ducks. She is one confused dog until she can relax when the recording comes to an end. Lad, who also lives in the house with Trim, just lies firmly glued to the rug in front of the fire and shows no interest in the television at all.

By the time my second lambing season came around at the Fawcetts' farm, in spring 1990, I should have learnt something from the fact that the starting date is always the first day of April — April Fool's Day. That morning an official-looking letter, addressed to me, fell through the farmhouse letter box. It was handed to me by the children, who were all demanding to be told about its contents. Richard was not at all curious at first, eating his toast and reading the newspaper as I took the letter out of the envelope and saw that it had the BBC letter heading. It was an invitation to appear on the *Wogan* show, and I was so excited that I went about my day's work in a euphoric state, telling everybody the good news. I discovered later that it was a hoax perpetrated by Richard, who must have gone to the most elaborate trouble to get the letter heading right as it had fooled me and everybody else who was not in on the joke. Although I felt a pang of disappointment when I discovered the truth, I was able to join in the laughter which was echoing all round Wensleydale after the story leaked out. To this day, I still get my leg pulled about it. As it turned out, I managed to get the last laugh because Lad and I did eventually appear on *Wogan* at the end of 1991.

I was still smarting from the April Fool episode when, a couple of weeks later, another letter arrived from the BBC inviting me to compete in the *One Man and His Dog* championship later in the year. I immediately rounded on Richard because I thought he was at it again, and it took him some time to persuade me that this time the invitation was genuine. I was more chuffed than I had ever been in my life because it had been one of my main ambitions to compete in that event ever since I watched it on television after seeing my first sheepdog trial on Anglesey ten years before. In 1984 I had approached Eric Halsall, the programme's commentator, at the North Wales Open Trials about the possibility of including me in the championship, but, after watching my unbelievably bad run with Sykes that day, with sheep all over the place and the dog ending up in the judges' box, he said he thought I would have to improve a bit before being let loose on the viewing public! Now, with the letter in my hand, I realized that I had made it at last. With no hoax to bring my feet firmly back to the ground I bored everybody by going on about it until they were forced to tell me to shut up or there would be dire consequences. But my friends were all pleased for me and, after I had won the competition, there was a big party in the village to which everybody was invited.

As soon as lambing had finished that year, Ian Smith, the producer of the show, arrived at Richard's farm with a camera crew to film me working with my dogs and sheep on home ground. The previous day I had bathed and brushed all the dogs so they were squeaky-clean and shiny, and I felt very proud of them that morning when they all came out to greet the television men, coats gleaming and looking every inch the pure-bred and intelligent animals they are. As we had just finished lambing, I was suffering from the bone-tiredness which always follows those busy weeks and I was not my usual ebullient self. But nobody seemed to notice this except me, and the filming went well.

I think the dogs enjoyed that day as much as I did, although they were a bit puzzled on occasion when they had to repeat a completed manoeuvre because the cameramen were dissatisfied with the results of their recording. For several hours we were filmed doing the type of work involved in everyday shepherding in the Dales – moving a flock of sheep along a country lane; getting sheep to cross a river; gathering on the fells; sending a dog to catch a ewe before treating her feet; all followed by the reward of a good pat for each dog for work well done. It fascinates me how the TV editors make such a coherent and interesting whole out of all the different sections of film they must have when they return from working on location like that – to do this is surely an art, and they must work very hard to get the required effect because the finished result was a pleasure to watch.

That was a busy day altogether because Dorothy Fitton, who edits the women's section of the *Farmer's Guardian*, also came to interview me. And then, after all the publicity and basking in the limelight, things returned to normal until the day arrived to travel down to Derbyshire for the competition. That was when the butterflies in my stomach began to go into action.

Bones — the friend who made the small gates for my first demonstrations with ducks — had taken a week's holiday and we all travelled south together; Trim, bathed and brushed, jumped into the car with alacrity because she had guessed she was going to a trial. There was a bag of dog food on the back seat and a metal feeding bowl, with a canister of fresh water for when she was thirsty. Then we were off, after almost forgetting my own luggage, to enjoy a week's competition at the highest level.

When the invitation to *One Man and His Dog* had been confirmed, I rang my parents to tell them the good news. They were over the moon about it, booking themselves into a hotel near the trial ground for the week. Every day they turned up on the field to watch the runs, joining in some of the evening socializing and, of course, being present for my moment of triumph at the end. I have never seen them so thrilled about anything before, and it was a lovely experience to be able to give them so much pleasure after all the heartache I had caused them in the past.

The filming of *One Man and His Dog* takes a full week, with the first four days for the heats, Friday for the semi-final and Saturday for the final. Everybody stays in local hotels, with all the television people and competitors — who can also take one guest each to give moral support — more or less taking the place over. One great thing about this sort of get-together is that everybody has similar interests and aspirations: despite the competitive nature of the event it was all very good-humoured and relaxing, starting off on the first night with a big dinner and reception for everybody concerned. What delighted me was that Glyn Jones was also competing that year. He was in the winning line-up with me when he won the brace championship, so I was in distinguished company.

When I arrived at the trials field, a stunning location on the edge of the Ladybower Reservoir at Derwentwater, I was pleased to find that the sheep being used were Swaledales. Trim is used to working with them every day, so the butterflies settled slightly for a time because that was in our favour. However, when I walked round to inspect the course with Glyn my heart sank again because the field was small, awkward and narrow. I knew this would provide a real test of both handlers and dogs during the runs, and that there would be little chance of getting the sheep settled down again if things went wrong. The butterflies started up again. Then I viewed the competition, decided I was hopelessly outclassed and relaxed once more, deciding that if I was unable to win the championship I would at least enjoy myself, do the best I could and perhaps do better another time.

Swaledale tup

I was introduced to Phil Drabble, the programme's presenter, for the first time but already knew Eric Halsall, the commentator, from times past when I had chatted to him on various trials fields. I was feeling quite comfortable with myself and my dog as I walked out to the post for the first heat, in which Dick Roper and Brian Dodd, two well-established and successful handlers, were my rivals for a place in the semi-finals. I really enjoyed the run — Trim worked like a dream, responding to my commands and working well at the pen, so I knew I was in with a chance. When it was announced that I had won the heat I was thrilled to think that I would be competing in the semi-finals on Thursday. I spent twenty-four hours in cloud cuckoo land, and then suddenly realized that the pressure was now on — if I could win the semi-final, I would be competing in the final. That I might actually win the final round never entered my head at that point, because my mind was in such turmoil every time I thought about the next stage which was looming ever nearer.

On the day of the semi-finals I was so nervous I was unable to eat any breakfast. When I took Trim out for her walk before going off to the trials field I tried to calm myself down, because I knew that she would sense my nervousness at the beginning of the run and this would affect her performance. But I did not have much success because Trim ran badly from the start – worse than I have ever seen her. There was no sign of my normally quiet, smooth-working, thoughtful trials dog throughout the run, although she became slightly more relaxed by the time we penned the sheep and we must have gained a few points there. I had chosen to run first that day and, after that disastrous performance, I stood on the sidelines with Trim to watch the other semi-finalist take his turn. I was joined by Glyn, who commented, 'If you ever handle a dog like that again, I'll disown you. That run was awful!' I had to agree with him, and we grinned ruefully at each other before turning to watch my rival's run.

I fully acknowledge that I won the semi-final that day by sheer luck, because the Irishman I was competing against, Paddy Roche, was unlucky enough to have an even worse run with his dog, Flash. So at the end of the day I ended up with the most points. In the *One Man and His Dog* competitions the maximum points for each section of the run are as follows: 20 for the outrun; 10 for the lift; 20 for the fetch; 40 for the drive (this includes driving the sheep away from the handler, the cross-drive and bringing the sheep to the shedding ring); 10 for the single; and 10 for the pen – making a possible total of 110. Points are deducted by the judges when faults occur.

When we checked our points after the result had been announced, Paddy and I found that we had been running neck and neck right up to the time of the single and pen at the end of our respective runs. Despite Trim's poor running at the beginning of the semi-final, she had settled enough by the end to achieve a single (although I lost 6 points on it because it was not a good one). Then she went on to do a good pen, but because of the earlier poor showing we ended up with a disappointing total of 91 points.

However, Paddy was unlucky enough to have a bunch of sheep which offered no opportunity for him to make a space for his dog to come through to single a sheep. He went over the allotted time of fifteen minutes for this stage of his run, and so the judges asked him to proceed to the pen. Paddy therefore lost all 10 singling points, and that is really what made the difference between me winning and losing – because, despite the loss of those 10 points, he still ended up with a total of 88. Had he managed a good single, I would have been out of the running. It was an event which proved to me, once and for all, that to be successful in competition there has to be a bit of luck somewhere along the line to give you a shove in the right direction – and that day it was my turn.

When I discovered that I would be competing in the final the next day I immediately made a decision to be sensible, go to bed early, get a good night's sleep and wake up fresh and relaxed the following morning. This, I felt, would maximize my chances of a good run. But all my good resolutions fell by the wayside as I joined in an evening of good food, drink and conversation with everybody else, finally dropping into bed in the small hours with the prospect of rising early to compete in the final of my dreams. To my surprise I slept like a baby and woke refreshed, looking forward to the day ahead and not one butterfly in sight.

News of my successful semi-final run had travelled fast, for when I walked on to the trials field that morning I could see among the spectators a contingent of friends who had travelled down from Wensleydale in the early hours to watch my final run. To see them all there made my day, and I was so grateful for their support that I decided I would have to give them the performance of my life as a reward for taking the trouble to be there to cheer me on.

Once again I was the first to run and, although I was competing against Willy Cormack, the well-known Scots handler with a formidable list of wins to his credit, I was only slightly nervous as I walked out to the post with Trim. This meant that there was enough adrenalin flowing to get my mental processes geared up for the competition, but not enough to paralyse my powers of concentration and reasoning. I am sure that Trim was feeling the same, because as I watched her confidently setting off on her outrun it was clear that she was in the same state of mind as me – keyed up to run out to her sheep, but thinking rationally and clearly. As my dog reached the top of the field and lifted her sheep quietly and smoothly, I relaxed and began to enjoy myself in the knowledge that we were both in good fettle and would be able to give Willy something worth competing against.

Towards the end of the run Trim came in to do the perfect single, knowing exactly what I wanted her to do before I even gave her the command. The final test, penning the sheep, was achieved without problems. I stood at the closed pen gate with Trim at my feet and my heart in my mouth, because I knew we had had a good run but not whether it would be better than Willy's which was still to come. When Willy's dog had a perfect outrun and an almost faultless lift I realized that, despite my lovely run, I could still lose the competition if he maintained that standard of handling – and he did! I am sure that I held my breath all the time until he had completed his run with a perfect pen, because I was quite breathless with apprehension until the announcement came over on the loudspeakers that Trim and I were the *One Man and His Dog* champions for 1990. Then I just threw my arms around her neck and wept tears of sheer happiness and exhilaration – without doubt the greatest day of my life, and made more so because so many of the people I love had been there to see it. It was not until later that I discovered I had won by only 4 points – my total being 103 and Willy's 99. Both were good scores by anybody's standards, and at another trial Willy's 99 could easily have been the winner. It was just that it was my turn for lady luck to take a hand in the proceedings on that particular day.

The Duchess of Devonshire presented the prizes, and I was in tears again when I was presented with my television trophy and accepted, on Trim's behalf, the winning dog's beautiful leather collar on its own stand, and the Sash of Honour which she wore resplendently at the big party we had in the pub back home at Hardraw that evening. And what a night that was, with champagne flowing freely and Trim behaving impeccably like the star she is.

I was in a daze that night, unable to believe that Trim and I had won the competition, and it took me several weeks to appreciate the full impact of our achievement. I still find it difficult to believe whenever I think about it, and there is no doubt that it was to be another turning point in my life – it opened the doors to so many other things which have happened since that time.

Following my success I made several television and radio appearances, including a programme from the Pebble Mill Studios in Birmingham which was broadcast live. That time I tripped down the steps as I walked towards the presenter, Alan Titchmarsh, and said, 'Ee, look at me, I'm just like a Grimsby trawlerman.' The remark dropped like a stone as nobody in the audience found it in the least bit funny — not a good start! But afterwards I went outside on to the Pebble Mill lawn to do a short commentary on the sheepdog handling of a four-year-old boy from South Wales, who was reputed to be the youngest handler ever to have competed in sheepdog trials. That seemed to go quite well, so I felt better.

Since 1990 was the Chinese Year of the Sheep I was invited to appear on the children's programme *Motor Mouth* at the BBC's Maidstone studios, demonstrating on the lawn there with sheep and ducks supplied by local farmers. The animals behaved well and so I could enjoy myself, knowing that children watching the programme would be learning more about the way sheepdogs work.

My appearance on the *Kilroy* show was a bit fraught because I was supposed to be appearing as a woman in a man's world, and found it difficult to go along with the assumption that women need to be aggressive to succeed in pursuits traditionally associated with men. I liked Robert Kilroy Silk, the presenter, and found him very sensitive, with a good sense of humour, but some of the other women interviewed really had their teeth into this 'battle of the sexes' idea and I could not go along with it at all. As far as I am concerned, women generally do better by simply getting on with the things they want to do — and this can be done without putting everybody's back up.

My friend Miriam Scarr accompanied me on this trip and sat in the studio with me during the programme, while Trim sat on a seat between us and enjoyed all the attention she received before and after the programme. Being a farmer's wife, Miriam found the hotel bedroom suffocatingly hot. As a result she was awake for most of the night and she really enjoyed having a swim with me in the hotel pool the following morning. Neither of us had brought our swimsuits, but at least we were modestly clad in tee-shirts and pants!

Trim was made welcome everywhere we went in London, until we tried to get into a taxi to take us to Euston Station. The driver at first refused to have a dog in his vehicle, saying he had previously had people's pets which had torn the upholstery or had tried to bite him. It took me some time to persuade him that Trim was a model of good behaviour both in private and in public. He gave in with a bad grace, and we reached Euston without mishap.

Radio interviews are usually less stressful than television, as I discovered when interviewed by Libby Purves. During this programme I met Victoria Wood's husband, the magician Geoffrey Durham, and a man who has invented a brick which can be thrown at the television set to switch it off — an intriguing idea which should sell well! I found the experience most enjoyable because the various people taking part in the programme were relaxed and friendly; Libby herself was very well informed, asking me all the right questions and putting me at my ease.

Compared to the long timespan during which I could prepare for *One Man and His Dog*, my appearance on *Wogan* was a rushed affair and presented an entirely different challenge for me — and also, as it turned out, for Lad, who was to appear on the programme with me. The BBC first rang me on Monday to see if I would like to be on the show. The next day they confirmed the arrangement. I was to go the studios at the end of the week to make the following Monday's programme, which was to be pre-recorded.

One of my first thoughts was 'What shall I wear?' As I was unable to make up my mind my friends Tony and Jo, who live just round the corner, came in to help me to choose my outfit. My next-door neighbour, Maureen, also turned up for the dress parade, firmly convinced that I should wear something really glamorous. She chose a low-cut and rather revealing black dress which Jim had bought for me some years ago — but that idea was thrown out when I tried it on and discovered that my winter layer of fat prevented me from getting the zip fastened. In any case, a black evening dress combined with a shepherd's crook and a sheepdog would have looked ridiculous — although it could have made a good talking point, I suppose.

Eventually we all agreed on my trusty tweed jacket, black trousers, Aussie hat and long leather boots. As my boots were muddy and my silk shirt creased, Tony and Jo, sighing at my lack of domesticity, took things in hand and did the necessary polishing and ironing to make sure that I would be presentable. My boyfriend at that time was Jiffer, a local shepherd; he took a couple of days off work and we travelled down to London by train accompanied by Lad.

My nervousness developed during the journey whenever I thought back to the telephone conversation I had had with Dad when I told him I was to appear on *Wogan*. 'Now do be careful what you say, darling, and try not to put your foot in it,' he had urged me, and I knew I would have his voice ringing in my ears throughout the interview. I was looking forward to a stiff gin and tonic in the hospitality room before the show, which would help me to relax and behave more naturally. But things never seem to go the way I plan them, and the minute we arrived I was whisked off to the studio to do the recording. A list of the questions Terry Wogan was planning to ask me was thrust into my hands, and I was told I would be the second person to be interviewed.

I watched the TV monitor while Terry was interviewing Tony Robinson, the actor who played Baldrick in Rowan Atkinson's *Blackadder* series and who, a short time earlier, had introduced an amazing programme devoted entirely to dung. Then it was my turn. As I walked over to Terry, I took a small Wensleydale cheese out of my pocket to present to him before I sat down. 'Sorry about the small piece missing,' I said. 'I got hungry on the way here and took a bite out of it.' It sat on the small table in front of us throughout the interview, and afterwards I heard Terry asking all and sundry if they wanted a piece of cheese. I couldn't blame him for not fancying it himself after I had taken a chunk out of it, and he probably threw it away as soon as I was out of sight!

For the first time in my limited experience before the television cameras I found myself quite unable to relax — partly because none of the questions related to what I had been led to expect from the piece of paper I had been given, and partly because, for the first time in my life, I was conscious of the need to make a good impression. To make matters worse, poor old Lad was totally confused when I called him to join me — he was waiting out of sight with Jiffer and could hear my voice coming from two places at once: from the monitor on the other side of the screen and from round the corner in the studio. In the end I had to walk across the studio to fetch him.

When he could actually see me he was fine and came running to me, walking at my side and sitting at my feet as I sat down again, at last feeling more relaxed and happy. But by then the interview time had come to an end and I was left with a feeling of anti-climax. However, I did eventually get my gin and tonic after the show and enjoyed meeting fellow guests Tony Robinson and Enoch Powell — the latter a man of great personality, enormous intellect and twinkling eyes who impressed me as a great character, albeit a bit crotchety at times.

A short time before appearing on *Wogan* I was interviewed by a woman for a local northern television programme; that too was a rather negative experience. She would talk to me, ending with a question. But as the cameras turned to me and I answered the question my interviewer would primp in front of a mirror, flicking her hair out and generally titivating her appearance. She took no notice of me until the cameras turned back to her as she asked her next question; then she was back looking in the mirror again. Every time I tried to answer her questions, I had to lean round in attempts to catch this woman's eye to get some sort of contact. In the end, I got so angry that I yelled: 'Oi! You're not blooming well listening to me, are you?' All the film crew laughed and cheered me on. I achieved the desired result by getting a bit more of the interviewer's attention, but I remain unimpressed by her technique.

I have now formulated a golden rule to follow whenever I am interviewed on television in the future, and this is to avoid all contact with the interviewer and typed lists of questions until the filming starts. I will then have no preconceived idea of what may be expected of me, and will therefore be able to respond more naturally and spontaneously to the questions. I might frighten my parents to death by putting my foot in it, but at least it will be me talking out there, not some insipid cardboard copy without a voice of its own.

12
DEMOS
AND
DISASTERS

In my second year of demonstrating with dogs I was still not satisfied with my performance. I felt that something was lacking, but I was not sure what it was until I saw Jemima Parry Jones with her birds of prey at an agricultural show. I watched, fascinated, as Jemima introduced and handled her various exotic and beautiful birds while giving her own knowledgeable and entertaining commentary which was relayed to the loudspeakers via a small microphone attached to her clothing. I immediately realized that more spontaneity can be introduced into a performance by doing one's own commentary. Since that day I have followed Jemima's example, talking to the crowd myself and being able to introduce surprise, humour and appropriate off-the-cuff comment. My demonstrations have become more relaxed and entertaining, because I can turn to advantage any unplanned occurrences.

The only problem is that the dogs get confused when they hear my voice coming out of loudspeakers in different parts of the ring, and they tend to move towards the place the voice seems to be coming from. This means I have to have immediate obedience if I am to keep them under control — and I am not always successful. Lad is the worst offender and will sometimes go up to a loudspeaker looking for me, but this always amuses the crowd so his lapses simply add to people's enjoyment.

Since I began to talk to the crowds myself I have been able to enjoy my demonstrations much more, because I can have a laugh and joke with the spectators — the more I get back from them, the more I am able to respond in turn. Tom Hudson, who is one of the top commentators at the big shows, tells me that my demonstrations work because I am a bit like a female Tommy Cooper, giving a professional act based on somebody who is unprofessional and makes a mess of things. I play on being a bit of a fool in the part of the show where I use ducks and things are always going wrong, but tend to be more serious when showing the audience how sheepdogs work with sheep; this combination seems to work well. Success in the show ring depends on good showmanship and getting the balance right, so I am always adjusting and changing things as I become more skilled at the job — and, like everybody else, I make mistakes which teach me more in five minutes of embarrassment than I could learn in a whole year of uneventful performances.

There was the time when, having put on too much weight, I practically had to pour myself into the only pair of trousers I had brought. By lying down on the floor, holding my breath and pulling my stomach in, I was at last able to fasten the zip. I then had a job to get to my feet because the trousers were so tight I was unable to bend my knees! Relieved to find that I could at least walk, I went into the ring and began my demonstration. But I nearly died of shame when I bent forward slightly and my trousers gave up the unequal struggle, splitting down one of the side seams. The television cameras were filming me for a future programme and I prayed fervently that I was only showing a leg and not my over-large backside as I tried to manoeuvre myself into a position where the affected side was away from the cameras. One of the commentators was heard to comment: 'Oh, that girl, she drives me round the twist!' I could understand why. Nowadays I try my trousers on before leaving home, just in case.

Other disasters have often added to the crowd's enjoyment. At one show there was a water jump in the ring for equine events, so I decided to use it and dispense with the portable pool I normally use. I worked Lad and the ducks through their routine, ending up with the ducks going down their little slide into the water — and then watched my lovely white Aylesburys come out bright blue from the dye that had

Aylesbury ducks

been added to the water to make it look attractive. The spectators love it when things go wrong – which is just as well when working with animals because they are not predictable. The *pièce de résistance* occurred when I went to Northern Ireland to demonstrate at a big event that was being held there.

Anne (J) travelled with me, and we had arranged to meet up with the Motor Cycle Madmen group who were appearing at the same show. The plan had been to join the men at Penrith in Cumbria and travel up to the ferry port in Scotland in convoy with them, but things failed to go according to plan and we found ourselves on the ferry at Stranraer with Lad, Trim, Queenie (a young bitch who eventually developed too much 'eye' and had to be sold) and my various props, but excluding the sheep and ducks because of the regulations regarding import of livestock to Ireland. The boat was just leaving the quayside when the motorcyclists arrived, tumbling out of their coach in time to leap about in mock anger, pretending to tear out their hair and then waving us a cheerful goodbye before going off to arrange to travel on the next sailing.

When we arrived at the hotel I sneaked Anne into my single room and then set off to find a mattress for her to sleep on, hauling it back from one of the rooms further down the corridor, making it up with some spare bedlinen I found along the way and fully expecting the wrath of the hotel manager to fall on my head when he found out — but nobody said a word all the time we were there. The following morning I decided to have my hair done to look my best for the show that night. Then Anne and I went off to do some shopping, only to discover that a bomb had gone off on the other side of the city and there had also been several bomb scares in the main shopping centre during the day.

I walked round the shops feeling really frightened for most of the time as my imagination ran riot, and I had to take myself in hand and give myself a good talking-to, as I wanted to give a good demonstration for the Belfast Big Night Out which most of the population of the city were expected to attend. The experience made me realize what terrible stress terrorism puts on the ordinary person in the street, and I always wonder how people can put up with it when it continues indefinitely on their doorstep, as it does in Northern Ireland.

The Motor Cycle Madmen arrived in the late afternoon, shortly before we were all due to board the bus which had been laid on to take us to the show site. This was a cordoned-off section of the main street in the centre of the city, a journey of only a few minutes under normal circumstances. But on this evening all the roads were blocked with stationary traffic due to the bomb scares, so the bus only managed to crawl about fifty yards before it was forced to a halt. In the end, all the demonstrators decided to get off and make their own way on foot. So, flanked by the Motor Cycle Madmen on their noisy machines and accompanied by Brian the clown, who was dressed as an English policeman and perched on stilts, Anne and I half-carried, half-dragged the props through the Belfast streets, expecting every moment to be our last.

If we had thought that that would be the end of our troubles, we were wrong. When we arrived at the city centre we were introduced to the farmer who had kindly agreed to supply ducks and sheep for me to use during the demonstration, and he proudly took us to inspect his charges. The sheep were Dorsets, which are usually easy to manage, and the ducks, although not as attractive as my own flock, were cheerful-looking brown birds which gave the impression that they would give little trouble. That was the night I learned my umpteenth lesson – never to go by appearances.

Before my turn came I was interviewed for Irish television. The interviewer introduced me as the famous lady sheepdog handler and trainer, and I think I managed to give a good account of myself in spite of the fact that I was shivering with fear since thoughts of bombs and explosions were filling my fertile imagination all the time we were talking. Then it was my turn to go into the arena, and a hushed silence fell upon the crowd who were expecting great things from me after the build-up I had been given. I set up the hurdles for my small trials course, sent Queenie off to round up the sheep and bring them down to me, then waited . . . and waited . . . and waited. Those wretched Dorsets had decided they would not move and Queenie, with too much 'eye', just set on them, paying no attention to any encouragement or commands. In the end, in desperation, I sent Lad out. The sheep immediately turned, walked quietly down the ring and allowed themselves to be penned with no signs of mutiny in their deceptively innocent faces. I could have killed them!

Hoping that I would fare better with the ducks, I set out the little course for them. With Lad at my side I signalled for Anne to release the ducks – and immediately wished I had retired from the show before even beginning my demonstration. The ducks, finding themselves free, just took off, flying all over the place and eventually disappearing over the heads of the crowd. That was when I realized that their wings had not been clipped to prevent them from flying. Anne told me afterwards that the farmer had been helpless with hysterical laughter, gasping that it was the funniest thing he had ever seen in his life before falling to the ground with tears streaming down his face. The thing which set me laughing was the look on Lad's face when his ducks failed to behave in their usual fairly sedate manner – he was dumb-founded.

As soon as the general chaos and laughter had died down, I went off with Lad to retrieve the ducks as best I could. One pair had waddled through the open doors of Liberty's (the shops had all remained open for the Big Night) and floundered into several rolls of flower prints. They were so terrified that they had defecated all over the expensive materials, and later I had to pay a substantial bill for the damage caused. When all the ducks — minus two who were never found — had been safely fastened up in their basket, and their owner thanked for his trouble, I announced to Anne that I needed a stiff drink. So we went off round the corner and found a lovely, old-fashioned pub where we spent a pleasant, relaxed half-hour away from the noise and turmoil of the show. But when we arrived back at the ring we found that Geoff Brownhut, the organizer, was frantic with worry and thought we had been kidnapped. I apologized for my thoughtlessness — it was one of those nightmare times when I could do nothing right. However, in retrospect, I enjoyed every minute of that time in Belfast and would not have missed it for the world, even if it did put years on me.

Would you believe it if I told you a story of a female dog handler who went off to a three-day show to demonstrate with her dogs — and forgot to take the dog who was the star attraction? I had been invited to demonstrate at the Devon County Show in May 1991, and so I set off the day before accompanied by my friend Susie Baker, with my dogs in the back of the car and sheep, ducks, props and luggage in the trailer. Susie and I were looking forward to an interesting few days in Devon, to be followed by several days' holiday before going on to another show in Oxfordshire.

When we were just south of Birmingham I was congratulating myself for remembering to put my vitamin tablets and ginseng into the glove compartment. It was only when I stopped at a service station for a snack and to let the dogs out to stretch their legs that I realized I had forgotten Lad. He was still in his kennel by the back door.

It was Anne (J) who came to the rescue after receiving my SOS call. Despite the fact that she has a large farmhouse, several children and a busy husband to look after, she dropped everything, collected Lad and was on her way to Devon on the first train the following morning. I got to the Exeter showground in good time for the first demonstration, but Lad had still not arrived. So I began by apologizing to the crowd and telling them what had happened, adding that I expected him to be at the showground for the afternoon performance.

As it was, he and Anne very nearly failed to make it — there was a fire on the railway line north of Exeter and all the passengers had to get out of the train to wait for a bus to take them the last few miles.

Anne was at her wits' end, so she phoned Dad, by now living in Devon, who turned out in his car to rescue her. When they saw that Lad had arrived the response from the crowd was terrific, and the applause at the end of our performance was so generous that it made the effort of getting him down to me worthwhile for both Anne and Dad.

Susie, a lively, extrovert and extremely independent young woman, was in her twenty-first year and suffering from terminal cancer when she accompanied me to the Devon County Show. Local people had already told me about her before we first met among mutual friends at a local pub a year earlier. We found we had much in common, with similar personalities and a shared sense of humour. There were other things, too. Susie, like me, was the fourth of five children; she had always been the 'difficult' child in the family; had never given a damn about appearances; had totally different standards from those of her parents; drove them to distraction; and left home on occasion before returning when things went wrong. The area where Susie and I differed was that she was unbelievably brave in the face of her illness, determined to live to the full the time she had left. I think I would have found that very difficult to do in her shoes, so I admired her courage more than I can say.

Her farming parents had divorced when she was sixteen, and she missed having animals around her. So she began to visit me to spend time with my litters of puppies, confiding in me that she would love to have a pup of her own. I would gladly have given her one of my young Border Collies, but she told me that the breed she was really interested in was the Golden Retriever. I decided there and then that I would give her a puppy for her next birthday, in June.

After being in and out of hospital for several months Susie had been forced to give up her full-time office job. But she still led an active life, spending three months at the end of 1990 working at the Low Mill Youth Centre in the small nearby town of Askrigg and joining in their skiing holiday with her usual enthusiasm and enjoyment. However, when she returned in January she was getting irritated at having nothing to occupy herself; that was when the subject of the Devon and Oxfordshire shows cropped up. 'I'd love to come with you,' she announced. We knew we would enjoy one another's company, and there would be plenty for Susie to do because she insisted on helping me.

Although Susie's mother, Margaret, made no secret of her reservations, explaining that it might be too much for her daughter to cope with, she did nothing to prevent Susie from setting out that May morning. She drove her over to my cottage and waved us goodbye as we set off at first light, although she must have had terrible qualms which, as it turned out, were well justified. Margaret is very honest and told me recently that she had preconceived ideas about my personality and behaviour which were both right and wrong. She thought of Susie and me as a pair of free, rather naughty, spirits — and still does — but now finds that I am much more thoughtful and honest in my dealings with people than she initially gave me credit for. I have made another valued friend.

I doubt if I have ever seen anybody enjoy themselves as much as Susie did during those three days at the Devon show. She was always at hand when I needed help, she went round all the stands, joined in the social life in the evenings and quickly made friends with all the people involved in organizing and running things. Everybody liked her and found it difficult to believe that she had cancer because she was so full of life and laughter. They told her they thought she was an extremely brave girl, but got ticked off for their pains when she told them, 'I'm not brave — pretty selfish really, just getting on with my life. And I intend to get as much out of it as I can while I'm still around. After all, that's what you're doing and none of you knows when your time will be up, do you?'

Oliver Edwards, the steward for the main ring, was so impressed with Susie that he decided to raise some money for cancer research during the show. A party of Cossacks, led by Pierre Pakmanoff, gave stunning performances every day, galloping into the ring at full speed and demonstrating superb skills on horses which were highly strung and difficult to ride. Oliver rode one of these animals round the ring without falling off and made over £260 which he gave to Susie for the Cat Scanner appeal at the Friarage Hospital in Northallerton, back in Yorkshire, of which she was chairman. This pleased her enormously, and when I was invited to demonstrate at the next year's show we spent a happy evening together planning for Susie to accompany me again.

We had been invited to spend a few days with my parents after the show. By the time we arrived at their cottage, Susie was unable to disguise her tiredness, but we all thought a few days' good food and rest in quiet surroundings would improve matters. We were, however, underestimating the problem and she was still quiet and rather pale by the time we were due to set off to the three-day show in Oxfordshire before returning to the north. My parents suggested that Susie should stay with them and wait for me to pick her up on the way home, but she insisted that she was feeling better and wanted to go with me, so we set off on the three-hour journey. By the time we arrived in Aylesbury Susie was looking very white and being sick, while I felt desperately sad and guilty because I had not insisted on leaving her behind.

'I'm sorry, Katy.' Susie smiled at me through the tears. 'It's been a marvellous week, and I wouldn't have missed it for the world. But now I'm afraid that I'll have to go home.' I think she knew then that she had had her last outing. As I put my arms around her I knew that, although I had known her only a short time, she was one of the most unforgettable people I had ever met. Her sister travelled down from London that day and took her home with her until her father arrived to take her back to Askrigg. For a long time I felt bad about allowing Susie to help me so much at the show; but after she died both her mother and her friends told me that she had really enjoyed being treated as a normal person and that it was the best thing she could have done. Margaret has said that I gave Susie the gift of her last week of quality time and 'proper' living – but that is nothing to the gift of friendship and understanding which Susie gave to me.

By the time I returned to Wensleydale Susie was only able to lie in bed, but she was still cheerful whenever I visited her and listened as I talked about the shows and sheepdog trials I had been to. What I really wanted to tell her about was my faith in God, because I felt that this could help her, but it never seemed to be the right time. Eventually I wrote her a letter on the subject, enclosing a copy of the 23rd Psalm, which I think is beautiful. Margaret told me that she and Susie's father had read the letter and psalm to their daughter several times and they were sure it had helped her. It would be comforting to think that it did.

Susie died in her mother's home, with her parents at her bedside, on 8 July 1991, one month after her twenty-first birthday – the time when I had promised her a puppy of her own, the time when most of us are looking forward to a healthy, happy adult life, the time when serious illness and death are things which only happen to other people. But Susie knew better. She left all who knew her greatly saddened, but enriched by having had contact with such a brave, vibrant and unforgettable personality.

Susie's funeral, at her mother's request, was to be a celebration of her life, with no black clothes or florist's wreaths — just bunches of the wild flowers which she had loved. Although I was in tears throughout the service and at the burial in the little graveyard at Askrigg church, it seemed more fitting, somehow, than Trish's funeral had been. I was very pleased when Margaret asked me to read the 23rd Psalm during the funeral service. Dressed in a bright red suit, which Susie would have liked, I managed to do so without breaking down, probably because I was at last able to communicate to Susie some of the strong faith which I had been unable to show during her lifetime.

Since Susie died, I have realized that she taught me to value the days as they go by, to cherish good relationships and to appreciate sound health, which is something we should always treasure while we have it. Susie had learnt that unnecessary unpleasantness uses up precious time which could be better spent, and that life is short and made for living. Now, I try to live each day to the full in the way Susie did, and rarely a day goes by when I do not think of her.

13
MORE PUBLIC
APPEARANCES

After the *One Man and His Dog* championship was screened in 1990 I realized another ambition when I received an invitation to attend the annual Women of the Year luncheon at the Savoy Hotel in London. There was no mention of Trim, who had partnered me in my success, so I determined to rectify this omission and travelled down to London with my dog at my side. The following day a limousine arrived to transport me from my hotel to the Savoy and Trim hopped in to sit by my side throughout the journey, watching the London streets pass us by as though she had been used to this sort of thing all her life. She also went through the revolving door at the Savoy without turning a hair and trotted quietly at my side as we went up the stairs to the banqueting hall. That was when we met our first hurdle.

'You can't take your dog in there!' The well-spoken lady was pleasant but adamant, until I told her that my dog was part of the invitation and that I had permission to have her with me throughout the luncheon (I was lying through my teeth, of course). She gave a resigned sigh. 'Well, I suppose it will be all right then. But you must put her on a lead. Oh, and don't let her fight with the guide dogs in there.'

Trim

It was my turn to be a bit snooty. 'My dog has never been in a fight in her life. Neither has she ever been subjected to collar and lead.' Then I relented a little. 'Don't worry, she's so well trained that she'll behave impeccably.' And she did, lying by my feet, sharing some of my poached salmon and not the least bit awed by the fact that Princess Diana was the guest of honour. All the national newspapers made a meal of the story, especially when I told the reporters that Trim had been refused entry at first, even though she was the reason I was there after winning *One Man and His Dog*. The story was splashed all over the newspapers the following day — marvellous publicity for us, of course, and a fitting tribute to Trim's achievement. When I attended the same luncheon in 1991 I chickened out of taking Trim a second time because the point had been made the year before — although I rather regretted my decision when Fergie came over to me to ask where my dog was this year.

After the second Savoy luncheon I was standing in the hotel forecourt with a friend and the commissionaire whistled for a taxi for us. My friend told him I had a whistle which could leave him standing, so he challenged me to have a go. Putting two fingers in my mouth I produced the loudest noise I could muster, much to the amusement of those watching. Even the commissionaire looked at me admiringly. There I was, dressed to kill in my black, thigh-length boots, black naval-style jacket, short skirt and smart hairdo — and then wrecking the whole thing with a navvy-type whistle. I enjoyed that!

Being a firm believer in using dogs for the job they were originally intended for, I have always been a bit holier-than-thou about Crufts dog show. It is aimed at pet and show dogs, with few real working lines amongst them. I must admit, however, that until recently my opinions were based on pure prejudice and not on seeing things for myself.

This matter was rectified when I was invited to Crufts in January 1991, the first time the show was held at the National Exhibition Centre in Birmingham. Anne (J) went with me and we set out in terrible weather. It was snowing heavily and there were already several inches of snow lying on flat ground, with considerably more on higher land. John said we were mad to go at all, but we ignored him and set off. Fortunately I had my four-wheel drive Subaru, otherwise we would never have made it out of the village, let alone to Birmingham. But after a few difficult miles down the motorway we drove out of the snow into blue skies, and we started to strip off layers of clothing because we were suddenly too hot.

We arrived without mishap at the Post House Hotel in Birmingham, where we were the guests of my dog food sponsors, BP Nutrition. The reason for my being at Crufts in the first place was to spend the three days of the show on the Beta Petfoods stand, giving away samples of the different types of food they produce and talking to people about the Beta products I feed my dogs. I had to sit under a huge picture of me and talked my head off (not difficult), signing photos of myself posing with a bag of Beta Field — the pictures went well, rather to my surprise. The high point was being introduced to Prince Michael of Kent, who told me that he had seen me on *One Man and His Dog*.

I did not have my dogs with me at Crufts, so when I was asked to do a photocall for the press I had to borrow a Border Collie from one of the competitors. Since that time I have awarded prizes to that dog, which has done very well in the agility field. His owner was a lovely girl who handled her dog with sensitivity and intelligence. As I watched them together in the ring I was surprised to find that I was enjoying the agility competition, although previously I had thought that training dogs for sheep work was the only worthwhile form of dog training. Working on the fells with sheep and dogs is an energetic occupation for which one needs to be fit and well; watching the agility dogs, I realized that those handlers, too, need to be pretty fit to keep running round the course with their dogs, while the training must take a lot of skill and patience. There is no doubt that the dogs love competing and are happiest when going round a good course, in the way that a working sheepdog is at its happiest when working or trialling. It is just a different sphere of activity for dogs and handlers which the purists say is an insult to the intelligence of the Border Collie — but there are not enough jobs around for all sheepdogs to be employed in working sheep, or to compete at sheepdog trials, so what else are people to do to keep their dogs active and enjoying life?

I have always been so enamoured of the Border Collie that I have never been much interested in other breeds, but Crufts changed all that. I managed to take a little time off to go round the benches and the rings to take a closer look at the many breeds, some of which I had never even heard of before. I was much taken with the Staffordshire Bull Terriers — they have amazing faces and tremendous characters, and I came away having decided that I would have one of my own some day in the future.

I went to Crufts again in January 1992, this time in a different capacity — Lad was appearing in the Personality Parade on the first evening. Only dogs of particular achievement and/or bravery are invited to this event, so I was delighted to participate with my lovely old, three-legged dog looking his best with a shiny coat and bright eyes. Also in the parade was Roger Haywood, Chief Inspector in charge of West Midlands Police Dog Section, with a team of police dogs and their handlers. Two children were with them — Jamie Walker had been pulled off his bicycle by three Rottweilers while riding in the park, and Martina Williams had been badly bitten when she tried to rescue her grandmother who was being savaged by a German Shepherd dog. Both the children had recovered from their ordeals and were very excited to be appearing at Crufts as celebrities. The RAF handlers were also there with their dogs, and there were some of the Queen's gamekeepers in their smart, tweed plus-four suits and tweed hats, with gundogs at their sides.

Each time I have been there, I have been surprised by the immense size and scope of Crufts and impressed by the superb organization and facilities. I was also pleased with the flexibility of the bar staff. There was a large notice at the entrance saying dogs were not allowed in the bar, but when the woman there saw Lad she said, 'Oh, that's all right, you can bring *him* in. I saw him on the telly on *Wogan* last week, didn't I? He's a star.' So in we went.

Another thing which I particularly enjoyed about Crufts was seeing all those people who loved their dogs and looked after them with no effort spared. Having seen the dogs tearing around the agility circuit, or parading in the beauty ring, I have finally decided that we should not become too precious in the sheepdog world. It is easy to think that there is no other dog worth having than a working Border Collie, but having seen so many beautiful breeds of well-behaved, well-trained and much-loved dogs at the greatest dog show in the world I have discovered there are many different facets to dog ownership and handling – and long may it continue that way.

At the end of 1991 I also went to the Olympia Christmas Show. I was ostensibly a guest, but was later roped in to present prizes to the agility dogs – most of them Border Collies, which excel in that field. I enjoyed that moment as much as I had enjoyed watching the three days of the show and meeting the riders and show people, many of whom I knew already from the summer demonstration circuit. There were parties every night, which was all great fun, but by the end of the three days I had had my fill of people and the bright lights and was relieved to be going home to Yorkshire and my dogs before Christmas.

Another great annual pre-Christmas event is the Smithfield Show, held in London. This great, bustling occasion is full of livestock of all kinds and their hopeful owners, who have spent the whole of the preceding year in preparation. If I could win a first prize there with one of my home-bred Swaledales I would die happy, but as it is I attend the show whenever I can, to look and dream and plan for the future.

I was invited to present prizes to the owners of the winning sheep at Smithfield in 1990. All the arrangements were well in hand the weekend before when I went to Catterick in Yorkshire to attend the Bedale Hunt Ball, which is always held in the Officers' Mess at the big army camp there. Being one of the area's major social events of the year, no expense is spared. I had a wonderful time, all dressed up in my lovely, full-length bright red silk dress, eating, drinking and dancing before finally falling into bed in the small hours, exhausted.

It was not until my head hit the pillow of the ridiculously narrow army bed in the room where I was billeted that I began to realize I must have had too much to drink. However, I soon went off to sleep — but not for long. I turned over in bed, and the next thing I knew I was lying on the floor in the pitch darkness with an excruciating pain in my left eye, my head spinning, and wondering where on earth I was. When I eventually found the bedside lamp switch I was unable to open my eye, which was already swelling rapidly. I quickly closed it again, got back into bed and waited for the morning, careful not to turn over in case I once again impaled myself on the corner of the bedside table. I was convinced that things would not seem so bad in the light of day and that my eye would have returned to normal by then.

Major Bill, the friend who had invited me to the ball, was horrified when he came face to face with me at breakfast the next morning. He whisked me off to the hospital, where I was told that I had scratched the cornea in addition to damaging the facial tissue around the eye. I was to keep the eye covered for a couple of weeks to allow the abrasion to heal properly. This meant that I would have to wear a small dressing and a patch over the eye, and I immediately saw great possibilities in my predicament. The first eyepatch the doctor offered me was a horrid pink thing which, not being a pink sort of person, I thought looked revolting. 'Have you got any black patches?' I asked, and was relieved when, with some amusement, he kindly obliged. Since I was a child I have always rather fancied myself wearing a mysterious black eyepatch, and I left the hospital feeling pleased with myself, despite the intense discomfort.

That episode was the reason for my arriving at Smithfield looking rather like one of the Pirates of Penzance, with my black eyepatch, black trousers, black shirt and jacket, and thigh-length boots. I thought the whole outfit was quite fetching and had spent anxious hours making up my mind about what to wear for the presentation, so I was a bit taken aback when I presented myself to the show secretary to get instructions. 'Do you *have* to wear that awful black patch over your eye?' she asked in disparaging tones. 'And I hope you have brought a skirt to wear for the presentations.' As it was impossible to take off the eyepatch (my eyes would not stop watering if I did) and I had only the clothes I stood up in, there was not much I could do about it all. Not that I really wanted to, anyway — so she had to lump it, and nobody else seemed to mind.

A couple of weeks later, when my eye was beginning to improve and I could dispense with the patch, I went back to Catterick to collect my pick-up which I had left there since I could not drive with only 50 per cent vision. When I arrived I went into Major Bill's office and, as I stood there chatting to him, there was an almighty crash. A huge pair of antlers, which must have been hanging on the wall for a hundred years or so, hurtled to the floor. 'Get out, get out!' shouted Bill. 'You cause destruction and mayhem wherever you go. I just can't stand any more of this.' So I fled, laughing, to the echo of Bill's laughter behind me.

My after-dinner speaking engagements have increased considerably since appearing on *One Man and His Dog*, and they are occasions which I always enjoy. The groups who invite me to speak represent all walks of life and occupations; they include Rotary functions, Young Farmers' groups, businessmen, Women's Institutes, Townswomen's Guilds and sheepdog associations. I never get nervous on these occasions and find I can be more relaxed and natural if I just stand up to speak with no preparation beforehand — this enables me to vary what I say according to the response I get and the questions asked. The show-off bit of me comes to the fore and I generally have a whale of a time — and my audiences seem to like this approach. After one talk a woman said to me, with relief in her voice, 'I'm so glad you're not one of those stuffed shirts who read from pieces of paper or cards and have as much humour as an undersized flea.' I took that as a compliment.

One of my most successful talks was at a retired businessmen's luncheon in North Wales. One of the organizers told me not to worry if some of the men fell asleep, because many of them had got used to an after-lunch nap since retiring. I did not relish the prospect of standing up to talk to a group of somnolent elderly gentlemen and so, after an excellent lunch with fresh salmon on the menu (a favourite of mine – and Trim's), I stood up to begin my talk. I started off by brandishing my crook above the table: 'This is a shepherd's crook, and I use it for hitting old men on the top of the head if they fall asleep while I'm talking.' So not one of them dozed off and they laughed a lot, joining in the spirit of things, enjoying the humour and contributing a lot to the occasion themselves.

14
ANOTHER YEAR BECKONS

When I first began to train my dogs, everybody said, 'Oh, it's just another phase she's going through. Once it all loses its newness and excitement, she'll forget about it and go on to something else.' But they were wrong. Now that I feel more confident in the things I do, especially in my shepherding, dog training and handling, it is a relief to know that at last I am capable of doing something really well in this life.

When I look into the distant future, I feel that all I will eventually want will be my dogs and some sheep, to work in shepherding, to compete in sheepdog trials and do some walking in my spare time. If I happen to meet a lovely man with whom I can settle down to a happy married life, buried deep in the peace of mountainous countryside, then that will be a bonus. But at present I am prepared for anything which comes along and have no set ideas on how I would like things to be for the next few years – although I do know that my sheepdogs will be a major part of my life until the day I die. I know that I have two fine dogs at present in Max and Trim, but I will also have good dogs in the future because my training methods work for me and should, with luck, produce great working companions again, particularly as my skills continue to develop. As Jim always says, 'Training sheepdogs is a lifetime's study', and I know that I will never stop learning.

Having become more involved with show people during the past two years, I find I like their company as much as that of people in the sheepdog world — for different reasons. I enjoy myself immensely, whichever group I happen to be with at any one time. Whilst the sheepdog world has taught me all I know about sheepdogs and sheep, the show world has taught me to recognize I also have another talent — performing before large groups of people and keeping them interested. I can also make people laugh and I love being in front of the television cameras. I am expecting to do more of this in the near future, and plans are already in the pipeline for various programmes and films.

After two years' experience in the show ring I am building up my demonstration routine considerably now that I have a better idea of what people like. Variety and humour are essential ingredients, but there will always be a core demonstration of the way a sheepdog works with sheep because that is what it is all about — I want to avoid getting too gimmicky and far from base, which would be a fatal mistake. So far, Lad has been the main attraction during my demonstrations, both in the serious side of working sheep and during the more light-hearted part when he is having fun with his ducks. But soon I will need to find other dogs to take his place.

Lad will have his twelfth birthday in 1992 and I will have to be careful not to let him get too tired. It is generally accepted that each year of a dog's life is equivalent to seven of a human being's, so in human terms Lad will be eighty-four in the summer of 1992! Demonstrating at a major show is hard work for dogs; not only do they have to give two performances a day throughout the three days, but they also have to cope with the stresses of hundreds of miles of travelling to and fro, sleeping in different places, a change in routine, and sometimes extreme heat. Lad is always eager to work and would go on uncomplainingly until he drops, so I am planning to limit his appearances in order to give him long periods of rest in between. What this really means, of course, is that the time has come to ease Lad into full retirement. I hope he will have a lovely old age, snoozing by the fire in the winter, stretching out in the sun in the summer, and leaving the work with the sheep to the younger generation. After all, he has earned it.

Kiri

At the moment I am completing the training of Kiri, an Australian Kelpie sheepdog, to add to the team. Slightly smaller than a Border Collie, she is quite striking-looking with her short, red and tan coat, pricked ears and bright eyes, and I have great hopes of her as we begin to work together. I bought her from Mike Csernovits in late 1991. Mike had become as enthusiastic about Kelpies as he was about his Border Collies and Guide Dogs for the Blind, and had watched Kiri's early development with keen interest. After the first-class early training that Mike gave her Kiri is responding well to the 'polish' I am trying to add, and I am sure she will provide a contrast to my other dogs in the show ring. She has far less 'eye' than a Border Collie, and I think she will lack the control and gentleness which my sheepdogs develop in their work with sheep. But she has an attractive, rather brash personality and there is no doubt that she will be an asset when working close to hand in the pens — the type of work for which these dogs are bred in Australia. Some Kelpies will bark while they are working (something a Border Collie should never do) and they excel with big mobs of sheep.

Kiri is no exception — sheep never stand to her (defy her) and she can always move them, although not in the smooth, deft way of the Border Collie.

The Kelpie has only been in the British Isles for the past decade, but it has already established a reputation as a fearless, energetic working dog and there seems little doubt that its use will increase as the years go by. There is some argument about the Kelpie lineage, but it probably goes back to the short-coated collies which were exported to Australia from Scotland in the late 1800s. A litter of very short-coated sheepdog pups is said to have been advertised in an Australian newspaper as being from a dam called Kelpie, a Scots word for a wicked water-sprite. As the breeding programme from these collies became established and they bred 'true to type' — consistently producing short-coated pups — they became known as Kelpies, a breed in their own right. But I am still of the opinion that the intelligent and beautiful Border Collie is the sheepdog *par excellence*, with his 'feel' for sheep, his ability to alter his approach to suit different kinds of sheep and to adapt to varied situations — which is why the breed is gradually taking over from other herding dogs all round the globe.

In addition to introducing Kiri to the next season's demonstrations I will have my two young dogs, Molly and Henry, who are of an age which will enable me to demonstrate how I train young sheepdogs. Both are level-headed youngsters, and by the time the show season begins should be far enough into their training to take differing venues in their stride as they go through their lessons in public view.

I have also acquired Trim the second — a twelve-month-old bitch from some of the same lines as Trim. So I now have a third youngster to run in the nursery trials when they start in the autumn, and hopefully Trim the second should be in her prime before the present Trim is retired. As with every young dog I own, or ever will own, I am full of enthusiasm about these youngsters and have great expectations of them.

Also due to arrive shortly is an eight-week-old pup — a nephew of Lad's with similar markings to my beloved old three-legged dog. If he has anything like the ability of his illustrious uncle, this youngster should be a champion of the future. So, although Lad's matings have never been successful, I will at least have another dog from similar lines to take me into the future. This pup's father (also named Lad) belonged to Mike Csernovits; shortly before he died, Mike gave his dog to Jim Hawkins – the man who bred my Lad and Jim's English National Champion, Cap.

Katy

Molly

Shortly before Christmas, I held the last of the year's ATB sheepdog training classes in Wensleydale. Then I went to join in what we call 'gathering the fells'. This pre-Christmas gather is done to bring the sheep down to the lower land for scanning – it is a time when we can sort the ewes carrying a single lamb from those expecting twins, after which they are kept in separate flocks until lambing ends.

There were five of us for the task in 1991: Richard Fawcett, his stockman Les, John Fawcett and his farm hand Nigel, and me. We were all crammed into John's noisy old Land Rover with our dogs. Richard, John and I sat in the front in relative comfort, while Les and

Nigel shared the back with their canine companions including John's red-coated Drift, who constantly growled and tried to pick fights with the other dogs. As we drove up the one-in-four hill towards Dodd Fell, John told me about an eighteenth-century monk who had walked from Hawes to Oughtershaw, at the far end of Dodd Fell, and said that it was the most inhospitable place he had ever been through. But when we turned off on to the old Roman road and I was dropped off at Top Pasture gate I looked back to Hawes through the bright, clear air and had to tell the monk that he was wrong – the sheer beauty of the countryside around and below me took my breath away and I felt as free as air.

The rest of the group and their dogs were dropped off after me at intervals and the gather began – a two-hour task which would bring us all down to the two lower pastures. I set off with Trim and Max, walking from Greenside (pronounced 'Greensit' by the locals) over the limestone plateau, my dogs racing over the steep fellsides to gather before moving the sheep downwards towards the fast-running beck. I carried on over to the peat haggs surrounding Bank Gill Head, crossing over the waterfall at the top and continuing down Bank Gill Side. This is the place where I sometimes catch sight of a resident fox which often shoots out of the tussocks only yards away from me, but there was no sign of him on this day as I whistled loudly to disturb the ewes, the red-painted hook and blue 'F' on their sides showing up clearly in the winter sun. I could easily recognize John's sheep because they have a red-marked horn to distinguish them from Richard's flock. Then I came level with the old hut on the field where, in years gone by, the shepherd lived and from which he would do his lambing, turning the ewes and their offspring back out on to the fell once they had lambed. With the fierce, long winters of these parts I wonder how any of them survived – including the shepherd!

Gradually the lines of sheep gathered by the five of us grew until they looked like distant streams of white water running down the hillsides. As I reached the old field at the bottom of the hill I dropped down to the beck and sent Trim to collect Richard's lot before he went back up to get the Land Rover. Then I carried on until we all met, with our sheep, down at the bottom. When the flocks had merged I shouted to John that I would count the ewes through the gate.

Nigel stood ready to notch up each hundred as I took my place behind the 10-foot-wide gate, holding it slightly open to let the sheep through as slowly as possible. The weight of the flock behind us pressed against the gate as the sheep attempted to get through the narrow space all at once. I had got to 785 when suddenly the gate fell away from the gatepost and landed squarely on top of me. I was flattened, pinned to the ground as the ewes trampled me in their rush to get across. 'Keep counting!' John shouted, pushing his way towards me through the mass of horns and wool. So I kept my head up as far as I could and did as he commanded, doing my best not to laugh and still counting away as he heaved the gate off me and helped me to my feet. In this job I can expect no quarter, nor enquiries as to possible injury – the sheep take precedence over everything, and that is the way it should be.

a mule gimmer -see glossary!

When all the sheep were settled and grazing in the two fields we made sure the gates were secure and left them there for the night, ready for gathering them again tomorrow to sort them before taking the flock home. We all got into the Land Rover once again for the ride back to the farm – with one dog less in the back because John's dog, Sam, ten years old and with a mind of his own, had gone missing.

The next morning I went to Richard's farm to see to the children, who were all up and reasonably organized by the time I got there. Joshua had lost his school book; his trousers were also missing; and then, when he found them, he was unable to fasten them properly because he was growing so fast. But things settled down, breakfast was prepared and eaten, the children left for school, the dishes were washed, and by nine-thirty I was once again in the Land Rover with the others for the ride over to the old fields.

After checking that none of the sheep had strayed we began to gather the two pastures, driving the flock towards Dodd Barn and the sorting pens. As I gathered New Pasture I found John whistling for Sam, who failed to return home last night. There was the dog, waiting for him behind the closed gate which always has to be opened to let him through as he refuses to jump, taking advantage of his age. We ran the sheep through the sorting pens — those with red horns (John's sheep) one way and Richard's the other. The strays which belonged to neither went the same way as John's ewes, to be pulled out later into a pen on their own. Most of these belonged to Ginger John at Swath Gill, and after the others had begun to drive their separate flocks down to the farms, I set off with the strays and put them into one of Ginger John's fields over the beck. Then I returned to help John with his flock, driving half of the sheep ahead but taking care not to catch up with Richard and his flock in the distance.

As I went past Debbie and Cliff Alan's farmhouse, standing at the edge of the road, I remembered several years when we were moving sheep during Christmas week itself, and Debbie came out with mince pies still warm from the oven. We passed Cliff's dairy unit and then, as the sheep wound round the corner in front of me, I saw that they were beginning to jump for some reason. Long John, John's father, had gone ahead and was waving a stick in an attempt to prevent the sheep from damaging the walls by Tot Iveson's field. His old dog, Moss, was joining in and I rushed forward with Max to help. We managed to make the sheep double back up the lane towards John's flock. About thirty ewes had jumped over Tot's wall but not too much damage had been done. We set off again with the whole flock, leaving John to gather the naughty ones from the field and shepherd them out through the gate before catching up with us.

In no time at all we were driving the sheep through Gayle village, over the little bridge into Hawes (the one seen at the beginning of every episode of the television series *Emmerdale*) and past the small dairy where they make the famous Wensleydale cheese. A little further on, we passed Hawes school, where the children were having their break in the playground. I could hear Josh shouting, 'I told you it would be Katy.' 'Hi, Josh,' I called, but he pretended not to hear me, going red with embarrassment at being the centre of attention, and turning away.

At the Crown pub in the centre of Hawes Big Dave rushed out, grinning at me. 'Come in and have a drink with me, Katy. Max and Trim can take the sheep the rest of the way on their own.' But I declined his offer before going past Terry the butcher's and Elijah Allen's where I buy all my groceries. I saw Bones's mother, immaculate in blue wellies, corduroys and anorak, out for a walk with Apple, the Jack Russell terrier I gave Bones for his birthday a couple of years ago. Then we were going over the bridge across the river Ure, past the football field and on to the Haylands — one of John's fields, where his sheep would stay until Monday morning. At The Croft, Richard's sheep had also been driven into the low-lying pasture near the farmhouse, ready for scanning. Now we could all look forward to Sunday pursuits before getting cracking again at the beginning of the week.

I was wide awake by six o'clock on Monday morning and, although it would not be light until seven-thirty, I took my dogs out for a long walk in the bright light of the full moon — the perfect start to what was going to be a busy day. John and his father were already in the sheep shed when I arrived, and we were joined at the sorting pens by Adrian Bell, the livestock scanner. We funnelled the ewes into the sheep crush where the scanning takes place, and as always I was fascinated as I watched the head and ribcage of a tiny lamb on the scanner screen, marvelling that science had made it possible for us to view the unborn foetus in this way. It took us two hours to scan six hundred ewes and, although a tiring job, it was much easier this year compared to past years when each ewe had to be turned over before scanning could be done. Now, they remain standing and there is less physical effort involved on our part, thank goodness.

With John's scanning done, I went off to Richard's farm where Adrian set up his scanner again and we were off once more. Les, Dick and I kept the sheep moving until, with a sigh of relief, the job was finished and we could all have a well-earned cup of tea. My four Swaledales had been put with Richard's flock after the gather last week and the scanner revealed that one was geld, one had twins and two had a single — and I had been hoping for eight lambs to swell my little flock this year. Oh well! Perhaps we'll do better next time.

Swaledale tup

Although I get such pleasure from my yearly contract to lamb Richard's ewes, there is an even greater delight in store for me when my own tiny flock of Swaledales produce their offspring, with the ever-present hope that at least one of the lambs will become a prize-winner later in the year. I have no problem in recognizing them individually as I chat to them during treatment and clipping. As with all the other animals I have owned throughout my life, my ewes all have pet names. The farmers around here probably think I am mad to give them names like Miriam, Anne, Pamela and Doreen. But the names seem to match their owners — and cause some consternation at times when I am talking about them, possibly referring to mastitis or dirty backsides, and people think I am referring to my friends who are their namesakes.

So things have come full circle and I am now looking forward to lambing time once again. Preparations are well in hand. My lambing bag has been checked and restocked with coloured markers, various medications, antibiotics, syringes, feeding tubes, a large penknife, stout string, small plastic lamb coats for use if the weather turns really bad and lengths of the ubiquitous baler twine which is put to such good and varied use by everyone in stock farming. Also tucked into a side pocket is a small hip flask of 'medicinal' brandy, which can be used to revive a cold lamb and also comes in handy to revive the exhausted and frozen shepherd on occasion!

I have a good waterproof jacket to take me through all weathers, stout boots and wellies which should get me through six strenuous weeks of walking without mishap, a sturdy crook, warm woollies, a balaclava and mittens in case the weather turns bitterly cold – and, of course, my dogs. I have already introduced a special supplement to their diet to help them build up the additional stamina they will need to keep them in good fettle throughout the coming weeks. This strategy works well because, although I always lose a lot of weight during lambing (I am always more streamlined in the early summer than at any other time of the year), my dogs rarely do. I put this down to careful feeding with the right food – and giving them two meals a day (rather than the customary one) when the going gets really rough.

Some time in the next week or so I will go into Holden's, the farm suppliers in Hawes, to collect my supply of ear tags engraved with 'Katy' on one side and 'Cropper' on the other. Richard and the other farmers all have a huge bag of these each spring to use as markers on their lambs, and have no difficulty in meeting the criterion of no orders being accepted below forty tags. As I only have four breeding Swaledale ewes of my own, producing a maximum of two lambs each, I only need eight tags. But as a special favour the rule is waived for me, and it always causes some amusement to see a long row of large bags with the various farmers' names attached to them, dwarfing my Lilliputian-sized bag at the far end.

One of the joys of this time of year is to spend all my waking hours out of doors with sheep, lambs and dogs, and to watch the winter turning to spring. Lambing in Wensleydale usually begins in cold, harsh weather, often with a last-minute heavy fall of snow, but inevitably the days lengthen, the weather becomes gradually warmer and I can begin to cast off my layers of warm clothing to end the lambing season in shirtsleeves. Easter always comes in the middle of my lambing stint, so I am never able to compete at the first Welsh sheepdog trials of the season, which are held by Glyn Jones at Bodfari near Denbigh every year at this time. By then Glyn's ewes have all lambed on his mountain farm and, helped by his wife Beryl and daughter Ceri, he is able to return to the sport which has given him so many years of pleasure and success.

The Yorkshire novice trials usually take place in April, so I can rarely attend those either, but the next big event is in May. This is the prestigious Fylde trial, just over the border in Lancashire, and I can usually compete at that, followed by as many other trials as I can fit in before the show season begins at the end of May with the Devon County Show. Following that, my attendance at trials becomes more sporadic, depending upon my demonstration bookings, but I still manage to fit quite a few in throughout the summer. Most of these trials will be organized by the Northern Sheep Dog Association, which has been in existence for over a quarter of a century.

The weeks of the English National Trials in August, and the International in September, are sacrosanct and I never accept bookings which coincide with these dates as they are the highlights of every sheepdog handler's year. There, I will meet up with all the friends and acquaintances I have met over the past years, catch up on the news and gossip, talk endlessly about dogs, sheep and other handlers, watch the runs, discuss the past and future of the sheepdog world, bemoan the difficulty of finding the 'right kind of dog' (always a favourite topic), join in argument and debate and generally enjoy myself.

But in the meantime it is still mid-March and my last big task before lambing starts on 1 April has been completed. This task was nothing to do with sheep – it was a sponsored walk which I organized to raise money for the beleaguered children of Romania. In common with everybody else, I had been upset by TV programmes and newspaper articles describing the plight of these sad children and was wondering what I could do to help. Then at a party I met Sam St Pierre, a retired dentist and husband of Sue, the vet at some of the big shows. Sam told me he had already taken a lorryload of medicines, food, clothing and other supplies to Romania and was trying to get enough money together to make a second trip. That was when the idea was born – a sponsored dog-walk covering ten miles of Wensleydale.

A friend who teaches at Leyburn Secondary School suggested I should give a talk to the pupils, as she was sure they would be interested in what I was trying to do. So one morning at assembly the headmaster announced that they had a special guest. I walked out on to the stage with Lad and Trim to a tremendous reception and a cheque for £346. I was so surprised and delighted with this unexpected gift that tears were in my eyes as I thanked everybody. After hearing my talk the pupils promised me good support for the walk itself.

When Sunday, 15 March, the appointed day, arrived I leaped out of bed at first light to find there had been a heavy fall of snow in the night. My heart sank, because I thought I would have to cancel the walk; but my worries soon disappeared as the sun came up to clear skies and a perfect late winter day. Being of hardy stock, none of the walkers were deterred by the snow. Well over a hundred of them, including many children, had gathered outside the Green Dragon pub in Hardraw, with their dogs, by the time we set off; the few without their own dogs took one of mine or Richard's. Our route took us through Hawes, over Richard's land to Burtersett, then along the old Roman road to Bainbridge and back to the Green Dragon via the old railway line. By this time, we were all wishing the railway was still working!

The walk was not without its highlights. We walked along the main road through Hawes, stopping traffic on the way and collecting donations in the battered old calf-feeding buckets that people had brought for the purpose. As usual, my lack of co-ordination came to the fore when I tripped over Richard's dog, Roy, spilling my bucket of money all over the road as I collapsed on to the tarmac helpless with laughter. It was also in Hawes that one little dachshund decided it had already had enough, so its owner left it behind with some friends in the town. Then, as his handler went over a stone wall, a big, rough-coated half-collie managed to get himself stuck in the stone stile.

Many of my friends, including Anne (R), were there to give a helping hand. Richard drove up and down throughout the walk, picking up people and dogs who had had enough. I brought up the rear, making sure that nobody had fallen by the wayside without being noticed, and hoping that I would not need to hold a memorial sheepdog trial the following week for those who had gone missing without trace.

When the sponsorship money was eventually added to the day's takings and the donation from the school we found we had made well over £1000. If we could raise all that money with a small, local event, we could raise even more if we could get more people to take part – and another idea was born. Why not make it a national event next year? That is something I can look forward to planning during the dark evenings of next winter.

The familiar excitement is mounting as I think of 1 April, bringing with it a lot of work for me and my dogs as we become completely taken over by the lambing task once again – as always, these are going to be six weeks when there is no time for any other activity in our busy lives. I know full well that before the middle of May I will be completely exhausted; I will be longing for a day off and the luxury of a long lie-in, followed by a leisurely breakfast in the morning and an evening drink with friends at the Green Dragon. But, as I watch the fields filling with lambs and have the satisfaction of a job well done, there is nothing in the world which could persuade me to give up the shepherd's life.

mule lambs

GLOSSARY

ADAS	Agricultural Development Advisory Service
ATB	Agricultural Training Board
AWAY HERE	Traditional command to send a dog to his right
AWAY TO ME	As AWAY HERE
BALANCE AND FEEL	The dog's ability to maintain the correct distance between himself and the sheep in order to control them. The actual distance varies from dog to dog
BALANCING	The dog moves quietly round the sheep, keeping them bunched; alternatively, he moves towards them, usually before moving or turning them
BECK	A brook
CASTING OUT	The dog's ability to run round the edge of the flock (to either side), ending up to the rear of the sheep and well back from them prior to lifting
CEA	Collie Eye Anomaly — a genetically transmitted eye disorder
CLIPPING	Shearing

COME BYE	The traditional command for sending a dog to his left
CROSS-DRIVE	The dog moves the sheep across the field in front of the handler
DAGGING	Shearing the back end of a sheep to keep it clean and to avoid infestation by maggots
DEW CLAWS	Rudimentary claws found on the front legs of dogs. Occasionally found on the back legs too
DOWN	See LIE DOWN
DRIVING	The ability of the dog to move sheep in front of him in a straight line
ENGLISH NATIONAL	The major trial at which handlers living in England run their dogs to compete for the top fifteen places. The fifteen then represent their country at the International Sheep Dog Trials the following month
EYE	The Border Collie controls his sheep by dominating them with his eye. Too much use of his eye can make the dog reluctant to move
FARROWING	A sow giving birth
FELL	An upland tract of moorland
FLANKING	The side-to-side movement of the dog when he is working sheep
FOG	A field containing long grass after the hay or silage crop has been taken
FORCE	A waterfall
GATHERING	A dog runs out to collect and move a flock of sheep
GELD	Barren
GILL	A small ravine; also a brook
GIMMER	A two-year-old ewe
GIMMER LAMBS	The current year's ewe lambs
GLORIOUS TWELFTH	12 August, the first day of the grouse-shooting season
GRIPPING	A dog using his mouth to grab the sheep

HOGGS or HOGGETS	Young ewe lambs before their first shearing
HOOK	The top of a sheep's hip bone
INTERNATIONAL	Fifteen representatives from each of the four national trials (England, Scotland, Wales and Ireland) compete for the coveted International Supreme Championship and other trophies
IRISH NATIONAL	The major trial at which handlers living in Ireland run their dogs to compete for the top fifteen places. The fifteen then represent their country at the International Sheep Dog Trials the following month
ISDS	The International Sheep Dog Society — the governing body for registered working Border Collies of British stock. The Society maintains a stud book and is responsible for the four National Trials and the International. It also establishes rules and guidance for affiliated trials throughout Britain, and is responsible for the eye-testing programme for Border Collies
LAITHE	Barn
LIE DOWN	The stop command. Some dogs will remain on their feet, others will actually lie down
LIFT	The moment at the end of the dog's outrun when he has his first contact with the sheep and moves them
MIS-MOTHERING	Lamb-stealing, which is sometimes done by a ewe which has not yet produced her own offspring
MOTHERING-UP	The lamb is suckling from the ewe and has been accepted by her
MULE EWES	Half-bred sheep which are very popular for the breeding of fat lambs intended for the meat market. There are two distinct varieties, and in Wensleydale they are North of England mules which are out of a Swaledale ewe by a blue-faced Leicester tup
NOVICE TRIAL	Usually for dogs which have not been placed first or second in a previous trial
NURSERY TRIAL	For young dogs to gain experience on the trials field — they should not have won an award in any other class of trial

OPEN TRIAL	A trial which is open to dogs of any age and experience
OUTRUN	The dog's run from the handler's side to the far side of the sheep. This can be to left or right
PEAT HAGGS	Areas of peat on the fells
PEN	The sheep are driven into a small enclosure, with or without a gate. Neither dog nor handler must touch the sheep
POWER	The dog's ability to master his stock in a controlled and fearless manner without going in to grip
PRA	Progressive Retinal Atrophy — a genetically transmitted eye disorder
RUDD	Paint used on the tup's chest to mark the ewes he serves
RUNNING ORDER	The sequence of runs at a sheepdog trial
SCOTTISH NATIONAL	The major trial at which handlers living in Scotland run their dogs to compete for the top fifteen places. The fifteen then represent their country at the International Sheep Dog Trials the following month
SECOND-CLASS TRIAL	Usually for dogs which have not been placed in first or second position at previous open trials
SHEARLINGS	Hoggs which have been sheared for the first time
SHEDDING	The separating of a group of sheep from the rest of the flock
SINGLE	Separating one sheep from the flock
STORE LAMBS	Lambs being fattened for market
STRONG DOG	This does not refer to the dog's physique. It means a determined and fearless dog which will stand his ground when challenged by stock
TAILING	Removing the wool from the sheep's tail before tupping time. Also done to twin mothers at the end of lambing
TARN	A small mountain lake
TUP	A ram
TWINED	Angry

WEAK DOG

This does not refer to the dog's physique. It means a dog which will turn away when challenged by stock. This type of dog may have difficulty in moving stubborn sheep

WELSH NATIONAL

The major trial at which handlers living in Wales run their dogs to compete for the top fifteen places. The fifteen then represent their country at the International Sheep Dog Trials the following month

WHELP

The young puppy from birth to the end of weaning

WHELPING

The bitch giving birth

CATS IN THE BELFRY

BY DOREEN TOVEY

Doreen Tovey and her husband bought Sugieh, their first Siamese kitten, to deal with an invasion of mice. They were not ordinary mice. None of the animals in this book could be called ordinary – from Grandma's tame owl, Gladstone, whose insistence on sitting on top of the bathroom door nearly froze the family to death in winter, to Blondin the squirrel, who chewed through a watch to find the tick and, when he was sent to stay with Aunt Louisa, insisted on sleeping, nuts and all, in her bed.

But none was quite so out-of-the-ordinary as Sugieh, daughter of Caesar. She was the living example of an iron hand in a small, blue-pointed glove. And when she had kittens, after a hilarious courtship and marriage, life just became more riotous than ever. Hardly surprising, with a batch of offspring that included the battling Blue Boys, a she-kitten named Sheba who was determined to be a Vamp, and the indefatigable Solomon Seal. After Sugieh's tragic death Solomon and Sheba stayed on in charge of the Tovey household, doggedly determined to keep the Siamese flag flying – and very thoroughly they did it too.

'If there is a funnier book about cats I for one do not want to read it. I would hurt myself laughing, might even die of laughter . . .' *Scotsman*

A Bantam Paperback
0 553 40588 8

CATS IN MAY

BY DOREEN TOVEY

When, after their hilarious adventures in *Cats in the Belfry*, the Toveys declared their intention of settling down to a quiet country life, they were reckoning without those inimitable Siamese characters, Solomon and Sheba. Fame went to the tyrants' heads. They appeared on television – and shook the BBC to its very foundations. Solomon took to making appearances in the grand manner with a Rex Harrison walk. Sheba stayed out all night and swore she'd been kidnapped.

The Toveys gathered other hilarious characters round them, too, both human and animal. There is Grandma, for instance, and her dumb parrot Laura (whose sad demise was caused by the coalman looking at her through the window). And Blondin, the orphan squirrel, who was brought up on brandy but later found furniture and trouser buttons more nourishing. There is the indefatigable Father Adams, once more uproariously involved in the Toveys' affairs. And the Rector, who becomes the owner of Hardy and Willis, two carefully chosen 'ordinary' cats. To his dismay, they prove to be of unmistakable Siamese descent. When the Toveys adopt Samson, another Siamese kitten, in the vain hope that he will bring out the best in those hardened sinners, Solomon and Sheba, the story becomes a riot.

'Unalloyed delight . . . A rare and precious talent'
Birmingham Post

A Bantam Paperback
0 553 40589 6

ONE DOG AND HER MAN

BY DIDO, ASSISTED BY CHAPMAN PINCHER

Chapman Pincher, distinguished writer on spies and the world's intelligence services, is also the owner of a rather special chocolate Labrador bitch called Dido. Or is it Dido who owns 'her Chap', as she refers to her human companion?

Here in Dido's autobiography, ghosted by Chapman Pincher, we are given an insight into an intimate and loving relationship. Trained as a zoologist, Chapman Pincher is in an ideal position to interpret Dido's view of the world and share her wisdom with other dogs and dog owners. Dido has much to say about herself, as one would expect in an autobiography, but reveals almost as much about 'her chap' in this touching and eloquent tribute to canine culture.

'Fascinating and hilarious'   *Daily Mail*

A Bantam Paperback
0 553 40439 3

A BOX OF CHOCOLATES

BY DIDO, ASSISTED BY CHAPMAN PINCHER

When Dido, the beautiful chocolate Labrador belonging to the distinguished writer Chapman Pincher, published her autobiography, *One Dog and Her Man*, she little expected the fame and fortune that would come her way. Her new-found stardom brought her instant recognition in the street and more fan-mail than her co-author, some from such salubrious addresses as Buckingham Palace and the White House.

In her second book Dido describes how she has lived with stardom, from posing for photo-shoots to signing her pawtograph, from opening fetes to opening her own bank account. Yet still she has found time for the great loves in her life: fishing, walking and eating, all, of course, in the company of 'her Chap' and 'the Boss', as she refers to her human companions. What's more, she tells us how she has coped with motherhood, producing the inspiration for the title of this second volume, a litter of seven adorable chocolate Labrador pups – her own box of chocolates.

A Bantam Paperback
0 553 40717 1

A SELECTION OF NON-FICTION TITLES
PUBLISHED BY BANTAM AND CORGI BOOKS

THE PRICES SHOWN BELOW WERE CORRECT AT THE TIME OF GOING TO
PRESS. HOWEVER TRANSWORLD PUBLISHERS RESERVE THE RIGHT TO
SHOW NEW RETAIL PRICES ON COVERS WHICH MAY DIFFER FROM THOSE
PREVIOUSLY ADVERTISED IN THE TEXT OR ELSEWHERE.

☐	40540 3	**CHILDHOOD**	*Bill Cosby*	£3.99
☐	40050 9	**LOVE AND MARRIAGE**	*Bill Cosby*	£2.99
☐	17463 0	**FATHERHOOD**	*Bill Cosby*	£3.50
☐	17517 3	**TIME FLIES**	*Bill Cosby*	£3.50
☐	40439 3	**ONE DOG AND HER MAN**	*Dido, assisted by Chapman Pincher*	£3.99
☐	40717 1	**A BOX OF CHOCOLATES**	*Dido, assisted by Chapman Pincher*	£4.99
☐	40399 0	**THE MANSIONS OF LIMBO**	*Dominick Dunne*	£4.99
☐	29306 0	**AVA: MY STORY**	*Ava Gardner*	£4.99
☐	13586 0	**SUSAN'S STORY**	*Susan Hampshire*	£2.99
☐	40424 5	**NANCY REAGAN**	*Kitty Kelley*	£4.99
☐	17245 X	**HIS WAY: FRANK SINATRA**	*Kitty Kelley*	£3.95
☐	13550 X	**DIANA'S STORY**	*Deric Longden*	£3.99
☐	13769 3	**LOST FOR WORDS**	*Deric Longden*	£3.99
☐	40411 3	**MOVING PICTURES**	*Ali MacGraw*	£4.99
☐	17512 2	**IT'S ALL IN THE PLAYING**	*Shirley MacLaine*	£4.99
☐	17239 5	**DANCING IN THE LIGHT**	*Shirley MacLaine*	£4.99
☐	25234 8	**DON'T FALL OFF THE MOUNTAIN**	*Shirley MacLaine*	£3.99
☐	40048 7	**GOING WITHIN**	*Shirley MacLaine*	£4.99
☐	17201 8	**OUT ON A LIMB**	*Shirley MacLaine*	£4.99
☐	17364 2	**YOU CAN GET THERE FROM HERE**	*Shirley MacLaine*	£3.99
☐	13824 X	**JUST SOME STORIES FOR ELEANOR**	*Stephen Pegg*	£3.99
☐	40588 8	**CATS IN THE BELFRY**	*Doreen Tovey*	£4.99
☐	40589 6	**CATS IN MAY**	*Doreen Tovey*	£4.99
☐	40354 0	**A DIFFERENT KIND OF LIFE**	*Virginia Williams*	£4.99
☐	40116 5	**ENZO FERRARI**	*Brock Yates*	£6.99

All Corgi/Bantam Books are available at your bookshop or newsagent, or can be ordered from
the following address:
Corgi/Bantam Books,
Cash Sales Department,
P.O. Box 11, Falmouth, Cornwall TR10 9EN

UK and B.F.P.O. customers please send a cheque or postal order (no currency) and allow
£1.00 for postage and packing for the first book plus 50p for the second book and 30p for each
additional book to a maximum charge of £3.00 (7 books plus).

Overseas customers, including Eire, please allow £2.00 for postage and packing for the first
book plus £1.00 for the second book and 50p for each subsequent title ordered.

NAME (Block Letters) ....

ADDRESS ....

....